KEY CONCEPTS AND DEBATES IN HEALTH AND SOCIAL POLICY

KEY CONCEPTS AND DEBATES IN HEALTH AND SOCIAL POLICY

Nigel Malin
Stephen Wilmot
Jill Manthorpe

Open University Press
Maidenhead • Philadelphia

Open University Press
McGraw-Hill House
Shoppenhangers Road
Maidenhead
Berkshire
England
SL6 2QL

email: enquiries@openup.co.uk
world wide web: www.openup.co.uk

and
325 Chestnut Street
Philadelphia, PA 19106, USA

First Published 2002

A catalogue record of this book is available from the British Library

ISBN   0 335 19905 4 (pb)   0 335 19906 2 (hb)

Library of Congress Cataloging-in-Publication Data
Malin, Nigel.
    Key concepts and debates in health and social policy / Nigel Malin,
Stephen Wilmot, Jill Manthorpe.
        p. cm.
    Includes bibliographical references and index.
    ISBN 0 335 19906 2 — ISBN 0 335 19905 4 (pbk.)
    1. Medical policy—Social aspects. 2. Social medicine. 3. Social
policy. I. Wilmot, Stephen, 1948– II. Manthorpe, Jill, 1955– III. Title.
RA418 .M326 2002
362.1′042—dc21   2002021404

Typeset by Graphicraft Limited, Hong Kong
Printed by Bell & Bain Ltd., Glasgow

CONTENTS

Introduction   1

chapter **one**   The third way: a distinct approach?   5

chapter **two**   Identifying the health problem: need or risk?   18

chapter **three** Responsibility and solidarity   32

chapter **four**   Consumerism or empowerment?   51

chapter **five**   Central planning and market competition   66

chapter **six**   Controlling service delivery: professionalism
                   versus managerialism?   83

chapter **seven** Community care and family policy   110

chapter **eight** Evaluating services: quality assurance and the
                   quality debate   123

chapter **nine**   Prioritizing and rationing   139

chapter **ten**   Conclusion   160

                   Index   165

INTRODUCTION

The study of health and social policy is at present characterized by sharply competing arguments, principles and ideas, and the fact that these oppositions and contradictions is one of the major features – perhaps *the* major feature – of this field. In order to understand the significance of the concepts involved we need to understand the nature of the conflicts between them, and this book concentrates on exploring those conflicts. Key concepts in health and social policy are studied through their juxtaposition to differing, and usually opposing, principles. And it is for this reason that the book title refers to key concepts *and debates*. Concepts and debates are inextricably intertwined in the process of explication of the issues under study.

However, there is a deeper logic to this approach. The juxtaposing of conflicting principles takes us into a tried and tested process of exploration and analysis, that of dialectic. Through the identification and exploration of contradictions we arrive at a deeper understanding of the two opposing elements in the contradiction, and we are then able to achieve a synthesis of the two elements which involves a more sophisticated understanding of the issues. Hegel and Marx argued that history can be understood dialectically, and that human progress is sustained by the opposition of contradictory historical principles, and by the resolution of those contradictions through synthesis. Marx's particular version of this principle, dialectical materialism, has lost a good deal of its credibility in recent decades, but the fundamental principle of deepening our understanding of reality through the exploration of opposing principles remains sound. It has come to influence important principles of adult learning, particularly through the ideas of Paolo Freire. In this respect, the process of engaging with this discussion is, as far as it is under the authors' control, shaped by the same considerations as its content.

The other important feature of this field is that the oppositions being explored here are the product of particular historical circumstances, which have unfolded in a specific way over the past three decades. If we consider some of the principles that feature in the book we can see that their importance to policy and practice has emerged specifically since the 1970s. In many cases the debates that are featured in the following chapters would not have been seen as worthy of significant concern or attention thirty years ago. For instance, the tension between consumerism and empowerment as frameworks for user power is, in terms of its importance to policy, specific to the last three decades. That is not to say that consumerism is new in a wider sense. The role of the consumer has been acknowledged and refined as a concept throughout the twentieth century, and it would have been perfectly valid to have considered the user of welfare services in the consumer role at any time during that period. But, during the last century at least, this was seldom done until the 1970s, and such thinking did not exert significant influence on practitioners or policy makers. If we look at the tension between central planning and market competition as ways of organizing health and social care, we see the same process. Market competition has been well understood since the eighteenth century, but in the UK it was not seen for most of the twentieth century as a sensible model for welfare provision. From the 1970s onward this changed, and market competition was taken seriously as an alternative to central planning. In this case, however, we have an extra element in the picture, in that a new idea – the concept of the internal market – seemed to resolve a number of contradictions that previously made market competition unworkable in a welfare state. Arguably this gave the case in favour of market competition additional credibility and changed the terms of debate. Something equivalent can be said about most of the debates which are discussed in this book. Thirty years ago, or even twenty years ago, most of them were not on the policy agenda to anything like the same degree as they are at the time of writing.

The crucial historical event that opened up these conflicts was the arrival in power in 1979 of a government which set out to bring about radical change in the British welfare state (and indeed in British society generally) and to reverse the direction that policy had taken since the foundation of that welfare state in the late 1940s. Margaret Thatcher's agenda was to achieve a cultural revolution which would transform what she saw as an over-collectivized, over-dependent population of state clients into a nation of self-reliant entrepreneurs. To achieve this, she and her supporters consciously engaged in a battle of ideas – something the Conservative Party had traditionally avoided as an activity more typical of the political left. The ideas which her regime promoted, and the opposing ideas which they were seeking to contest, provide much of the material which forms the basis of this book. She promoted individual responsibility against social solidarity. Consumerism arose out of her conception of the role of the individual in the market-oriented society, whereas the concept of empowerment, with its associations with the radical left, was anathema to her. She consistently valued managers above professionals in most spheres. Her approach to community care reflected an emphasis on family care which expressed an attachment to the traditional role of women. Her emphasis on value for money in the welfare state stimulated the development of quality assurance; and her commitment to reducing state expenditure stimulated greater openness on the issue of prioritizing and rationing. So this book can be seen as taking up the contradictions that the Conservative governments of 1979 onward placed on the agenda. In retrospect it is clear that the ideological position favoured by the Thatcher government did not always determine the creation of policy; that the changes wrought in the machinery of health and social care did not express in full the ideological aspirations of Margaret Thatcher and her supporters; and that contemporary perceptions of an all-encompassing revolution are not borne out in retrospect. In many ways the changes were limited, sometimes to the frustration of those seeking to carry them through. The historical distance available at the time of writing allows us to take that into account. But while it did not always make the practical changes it wanted, the Conservative government did succeed in opening up the questions, which remain open.

However, this discussion is not simply an exercise in surveying the policy arguments of the 1980s and 1990s. It is also concerned with the task of successor governments in moving forward from the issues that they inherited. At the time of writing a Labour government is in power, with an agenda that includes the continuation of some elements of the Conservative legacy, and the reversal of others. However, this government clearly does not see itself as having a simple choice between what to accept of the previous regime's heritage and what to reverse. In that respect it seems to be attempting to break out of the previous pattern of party alternation in government, and is trying instead to transcend the simplistic left versus right configuration of some of the debates concerned. Moreover, the present government seems to be attempting to find a way forward that goes beyond taking up a position equidistant between the opposing positions. It is open to question whether the 'third way' set out by New Labour is in fact anything more than the finding of an intermediate location. In the case of the National Health Service (NHS), for example, the Labour government has retained the commissioner/provider distinction, but has replaced market competition with a duty of cooperation. Does this involve anything more than a mixture of 'keep some, change some' from the previous government? Is it possible, in the confines of British politics, to go beyond that response and truly to find a way of transcending the existing dichotomies?

The authors have not attempted to answer these questions on a case-by-case level, but have sought to offer a level of reflection on the opposing arguments that helps the reader to consider ways forward in policy terms. The authors have also attempted to identify some of the social and cultural changes that have emerged in recent decades alongside the policy debates. The individualization of culture, the changes in gender relations and in social institutions such as the family and the community, and the extensive changes in the nature of and experience of work, all have major implications for the development of health and social policy, in terms of what is needed and what is possible. To some degree these represent the context of the debates, but it is also the case that social and health policies over the past three decades have helped to mould and shape culture and daily living. So in a real sense the policy and social levels interact with one another. The prospects and possibilities of policy over the next few years will clearly be affected by the kind of society and culture that has taken shape, and the kind of context it provides for policy development.

chapter one

THE THIRD WAY:
A DISTINCT APPROACH?

Introduction

This chapter analyses the definition and conceptual background to third way politics and social provision. It discusses New Labour's association with the third way by reference to specific social policy areas, for example health, income maintenance and community neighbourhood regeneration, and in doing so attempts to identify parallels with previous so-called doctrinal debates, such as the role of state versus market in health and social provision.

The third way

Giddens (1998: 64) in his book *The Third Way: The Renewal of Social Democracy* states: 'The overall aim of third way politics should be to help citizens pilot their way through the major revolutions of our time: globalisation, transformations in personal life and our relationship to nature.' The claim is that the neo-liberals want to shrink the state, and that the social democrats, historically, have been keen to expand it. The third way argues that what is necessary is to reconstruct it. This in turn involves devolution, 'double democratisation' (Giddens 1998: 70–8), the renewal of the public sphere, administrative efficiency and more direct democracy.

The politics of the third way is evaluated in several sources, each attempting to distinguish it from the old left and the Conservative right, for example Giddens 1994, 1998; Miliband 1994; Wright 1996; Labour

Party 1997; Le Grand 1998; Driver and Martell 1999; Hay 1999; Powell 1999. Giddens portrays the third way as a form of modernized social democracy, a distinctive political territory focused upon inclusivity. Others, for example, Driver and Martell (1999) and Le Grand (1998) contrastingly view it more non-ideologically as a set of values and ideas bound together for pragmatic purposes to drive forward policy and to engender a sense of community and social responsibility.

Driver and Martell (1999) analyse the roots of New Labour welfare policy, its origins and characteristics, and associate the third way with a culmination process resulting from attempts to modernize old Labour strategies. Giddens (1998: 25) suggests that the phrase originated at the turn of the century and was popular among right-wing groups in the 1920s: 'In the early post-war period, social democrats quite explicitly thought of themselves as finding a way distinct from American market capitalism and Soviet communism.' He quotes the example of Swedish social democrats during the late 1980s who emphasized 'programmatic renewal'. However, a contemporary view is that the third way is no more than an extension of neo-liberal, post-Thatcherite politics (e.g. Hutton 1999).

An assertion has been that the third way draws upon ideas from communitarianism (Etzioni 1993), particularly with regard to notions of ending welfare and building community. According to Etzioni (1993: 2)

> The Communitarian assertions rest upon a single core thesis: Americans – who have long been concerned with the deterioration of private and public morality, the decline of the family, high crime rates, and the swelling of corruption in government – can now act without fear. We can act without fear that attempts to shore up our values, responsibilities, institutions and communities will cause us to charge into a dark tunnel of moralism and authoritarianism that leads to a church-dominated state or a right-wing world.

Of principal concern is stress upon re-establishing a link between rights and responsibilities with recognition that some responsibilities do not entail rights. Values of communitarianism refer to adjusting some rights to changed circumstances in the demand for 'civil renewal' (1993: 89–116). Whereas Etzioni does not allude to the third way directly, his attempt to conjure up an alternative to left–right politics concurs with those who have identified a need to construct a more coherent framework as a response to modern social change. Looking for theoretical flesh to be put on the skeleton of third way policy making has clustered around what Giddens has called the 'common morality of citizenship'. This denotes a narrative concerning responsibilities as much as rights. In terms of New Labour politics the pragmatic character of the third way is stressed more, i.e. the theme of managing change: 'accept the challenge of the future but refuse to consider ourselves powerless to overcome it' (Blair 1998).

Giddens has argued that reform of the state and government should be a basic orienting principle of third way politics – a process of the deepening and widening of democracy. Government can act in partnership with agencies in civil society to foster community renewal and development involving an extension of the market economy. He refers to third way politics as one nation politics promoting social inclusion but also with a key role in fostering 'transnational systems of governance' (1998: 69). Giddens emphasizes the third way as being a response to the dangers and advantages of a 'new risk environment' (1998: 70). The work of Beck (1992) is alluded to, where it is argued that the definition and management of risk permeates modern society. Beck (1992: 21) claims that early modern industrial society was characterized by industrialized production and individuals' life experiences were related to their access to benefits created, especially wealth. However, increasingly industrial production and modernization are generating not only positive benefits such as wealth but also hazards. Thus individuals' life experiences are increasingly related to the extent to which they are exposed to the hazards and risks of modern society.

Giddens (1998: 70) identifies a programme in the making:

The third way programme

The radical centre
The new democratic state (the state without enemies)
Active civil society
The democratic family
The new mixed economy
Equality as inclusion
Positive welfare
The social investment state
The cosmopolitan nation
Cosmopolitan democracy

Accordingly, he argues that the debate over the future of social democracy during the last ten to fifteen years has raised a diversity of general questions and created five specific dilemmas:

- *Globalization*: nations retain considerable governmental, economic and cultural power over their citizens but they will often only be able to wield such powers in active collaboration with one another, with their own localities and regions.
- *Individualism*: the rising importance of individualism and lifestyle diversity requires a new relationship between individual and government. The rise of market economies, fragmentation and deregulation

has made individuals more vulnerable and allocation of blame more complex.

- *Left and right*: this distinction is not exhausted but a fundamental question is whether the division covers as much of the political field as it used to do. A range of problems have come to the foreground that are not within the reach of the left–right scheme such as ecological questions, and issues to do with the changing nature of family, work, personal and cultural identity.
- *Political agency*: this involves a rethink of what government can achieve, e.g. to reconcile the divergent claims of special interest groups both in practice and in law. This relates to the declining trust in politicians and the machinery of orthodox politics.
- *Ecological issues*: science and technology have become integral to politics but characteristically experts disagree, hence the dilemma involves the nature of our relationship to scientific advance and our response to risk.

The third way and New Labour

Powell (1999) has examined the extent to which New Labour policies tend more towards a continuation of Old Labour, a convergence with the New Right or a distinctive third way. His assessment demonstrates a lack of clarity regarding the general direction of Labour's politics. Nevertheless, the claim by New Labour is that values have not changed but are placed within a modern context and that the third way returns to human values of the left – justice, solidarity, freedom. The rethink is around mode of delivery and the context is described as 'post-ideological'. Tony Blair's Fabian Society article (1998) presents a descriptive analysis of the third way, setting out plans for the future and focusing upon different areas of social policy.

When New Labour came to power in 1997 the claim was that its policies represented third way politics. The question is, do they demonstrate evidence of substantive difference? Certainly references to the third way peppered the Prime Minister's speeches during Labour's first year in government; yet some critics soon latched on to the notion that this could be merely a smokescreen for defending the capitalist status quo (Hutton 1998). This entails the view that the third way could be seen as amounting to a philosophy of social liberalism, in which the structures and inequalities of British market capitalism are taken as a given but the state tries to alleviate the worst effects without seriously challenging the interests of the advantaged.

The idea of 'social exclusion' is an example of New Labour analysis around the notion of those who pay for and those who benefit from the welfare state. In this case the emphasis is upon managing policies directed towards creating equality of opportunity rather than towards equality of outcome. Le Grand (1982, 1990) had claimed much earlier that the welfare state was actually less focused upon redistribution than upon featherbedding the middle classes, especially through health and education. In line with this judgement New Labour's efforts to reform the tax and benefit system have not intended radical changes but further means testing, emphasizing reducing welfare dependency and creating incentives to find work chiefly through extending educational opportunity. Labour's welfare-to-work programme is heavily targeted on the young and long-term unemployed and on lone parents. Labour's Policy Review (Labour Party 1996) attempted to shed the 'tax and spend' image and subordinated welfare reform to economic policy priorities. Powell (1999) claims that this represented the culmination of a gradual development of the scope of Labour's policies for welfare while in opposition. The Social Exclusion Unit (1998) stressed causes rather than effects. It asserted that the New Deals for the unemployed, lone parents and disabled people, together with the government's actions on failing schools, crime reduction and public health, represented a watershed in terms of starting to address the major causes of social exclusion rather than just dealing with its effects.

In the report A New Contract for Welfare: New Ambitions for our Country (DSS 1998: 31), under the section 'Responsibilities and Rights' it is stated:

> The responsibilities of individuals who can provide for themselves and their families to do so must always be matched by a responsibility on the part of Government to provide opportunities for self-advancement (para. 38) . . .
> The Government's commitment to expand significantly the range of help available therefore alters the contract with those who are capable of work (para. 39).

Making work pay becomes the cornerstone, introducing, for example, the Working Families Tax Credit and the Childcare Tax Credit in October 1999:

> The new welfare state should help and encourage people of working age to work where they are capable of doing so. The Government's aim is to rebuild the welfare state around work.
>
> (DSS 1998: 23)

Frank Field, appointed to head social security reform following the 1997 election, stressed the purpose of the welfare state as being to assist individuals in helping themselves out of dependency on the welfare state. That is to say it should be less redistributional and more focused upon the universalist character of 'stakeholder' social insurance covering social security and pensions. Field, even since his departure one year later from ministerial office, continued to argue the morally damaging effects of welfare dependency upon individuals. This idea has been largely subscribed to by New Labour although in practice welfare reforms have meant increased targeting and means testing at the lower end of income scales. The Social Exclusion Unit places an onus upon local experiment in developing new ways of creating work and improving welfare; Field himself was in favour of giving local social security offices more autonomy and power of discretion over administrative budgets, although not benefit levels. Its guiding principles are that those able-bodied persons who can help themselves out of dependence on the welfare state to independence have an obligation to do so. Only those who cannot help themselves merit special help.

New Labour third way politics has purportedly endeavoured to reclaim the public service principle while not confusing this with old models of public service organization and delivery (Wright 1996). In health and education many of the basic structures appear to remain unchanged. Policies implicitly accept the free market to deliver services but this is tempered by centralized regulation: for instance, the state will intervene in the case of deficient performance, or to stimulate market forces, or when it perceives refusal by any local service to modernize. To take the example of the National Health Service, on 9 December 1997 the Labour government published its White Paper for the NHS in England, entitled *The New National Health Service: Modern, Dependable* (DoH 1997). In the foreword, the Prime Minister stated that 'creating the NHS was the greatest act of modernisation ever achieved by a Labour Government'. Given the importance laid by New Labour on the term 'modernization', this was an important statement (Paton 1999). In evidence for sustaining the public service principle, the White Paper laid emphasis on the state, urging greater partnership between planners and providers, and performance accountability. As such the internal market was to be abandoned as it was perceived to foster a two-tier system and involve heavy administrative and transactional costs (these were to be cut to allow more resources for 'front-line' patient care).

The main change in practice for the NHS, however, has been from 1 April 1999 to entrust primary care groups (PCGs), instead of health authorities, to commission provision. Health authorities, expected to become fewer in number through mergers over time, henceforth were to take fundamental responsibility for planning services, i.e. strategic decisions for hospital closure and reprovision. Making GPs responsible for commissioning would also end the criticism that the distinction between fundholding and non-fundholding GPs created a two-tier service. When passed into legislation, the effects of the new White Paper would crucially depend on how much the new PCGs were taking the powers of the health authority (Paton 1999: 59). An early paragraph in the White Paper stated that there will be no return to the 'command and control' of the NHS which had existed prior to the Conservatives' reforms. Somewhat typical of New Labour's approach, however, National Service Frameworks (NSFs) were imposed upon the NHS as on other areas of social provision. This demonstrated continuity with the general direction of Conservative reforms during the early to mid-1990s (for example the NHS and Community Care Act 1990), giving added prominence to performance management from above and announcement of commissions to police the NHS through the National Institute for Clinical Excellence (NICE) and the Commission for Health Improvement (CHImp). The first was to be responsible for 'service frameworks' in all specialities, which would identify appropriate forms of treatment and appropriate ways of delivering that treatment. The second was to be deployed to enforce standards. Poorly performing trusts, for example, would be inspected and subjugated if necessary, hence centralized surveillance would be the means for enforcing good performance.

The third way, modernization and social provision

Reforming the Conservative reforms in health, social services, education and social security has become the principal approach adopted by New Labour politicians. A main difference is that standards can be raised in the last instance by government authorization instead of through market forces. The earlier doctrinal debates – individual versus collective, public versus private, state versus market, hospital versus community – are gradually becoming supplanted, resulting in recognition of the interdependence of these concepts and their subsequent interpretation into policy action. An underlying premise in government dialogue is that inequalities are rooted in the lack of individual skills and the inability to compete and that commensurate preventative action should be the basis of both national and local service planning. The moral objective of reclaiming personal responsibility and building an awareness of community are endemic to new plans despite what already seems a lack of effective means for putting such plans into practice.

Johnson (1999), writing on New Labour reform of personal social services, points to the fact that relative to other domains, for example welfare-to-work, this area has received little attention. The White Paper *Modernising Social Services* (DoH 1998, November) established a social services modernization fund and made reference to the third way, described as focusing on 'the quality of services experienced by, and outcomes achieved for, individuals and their carers and families'. It is based on seven key principles:

- care provided in a way which supports independence and dignity;
- services that meet individuals' specific needs in a coordinated way;
- care that is delivered in a fair and consistent way in every part of the country;
- care for children that gives them a decent start in life;
- safeguards for adults and children against abuse by the services;
- care provided by a trained and skilled workforce;
- assured standards of care from local services.

A statutory duty was to be laid on local authorities and health authorities to work together to promote the well-being of their local communities. The primary antecedent to this is the 1974 reorganization of the NHS and local government which placed on both sets of authority a statutory duty to collaborate through a joint consultative committee (JCC), later widened to include the voluntary sector. A difference is that the 1998 White Paper places partnership in the foreground and identifies the NHS, housing, criminal justice agencies, education, the employment service, the voluntary sector and, significantly, users, carers and their representatives as of equal significance in establishing and sustaining partnerships. It has been questioned whether this approach is likely to offer user empowerment and whether social services will emerge as an equal partner with other agencies as a result (Davis 1999; Wistow 2000). The suggestion is that the White Paper retains a prime focus on managing limited and targeted provision for the poor rather than seeking to work in a more participatory way with diverse and marginalized user groups. The tone reinforces the welfare to work ethos by appearing to maintain a distinction between the deserving and the non-deserving poor.

At rhetorical level New Labour's message has striven to build upon the importance of community. Where Old Labour looked to the state for action, New Labour talks of reinventing government through collective action in the community (Driver and Martell 1999: 27–8). For example, the initial strategy for mental health was described as navigating a 'third way' – somewhere between the old approach of institutionalizing people and the current, much criticized, policy of care in the community introduced by the Conservatives (Snell 1998). Of precedence has been the development of strategy which is proactive towards establishing a framework for care in the community. The detail is around increasing the number of acute short stay psychiatric beds and improved support for seriously ill clients and their carers at home through initiatives such as home treatment and assertive outreach. Round-the-clock crisis helplines were to be set up, with crisis teams, including social workers, on call

24 hours a day. An intention of the new NSF is to recruit more staff and have training and workforce planning at its core. Significantly this marks a shift towards better resourcing but is also an explicit recognition of communities as vital units of social organization adding to the significance of community care. Johnson (1999: 92) suggests that communitarian philosophy emphasizing duties, responsibility and civic obligation will push the voluntary sector further to centre stage as the market economy of care develops.

The 'stick and carrot' approach towards improving public services has become evident in New Labour's attitude to strengthening the family and its role in bringing children up to become self-reliant individuals and good citizens. A return to traditional family values, reversing the 'parental deficit', has hallmarked several policies. Whereas the previous approach had sustained a tenor of laissez-faire, affirming family values as an excuse for withdrawal of state support, the current approach stresses intervention, for example introducing moral education into the school curriculum. There has been no reversal of Conservative reforms within social care, health or education but an expressed intention to modernize. In educational policy, the third way has emphasized radical experimentation in partnership between industry, local education authorities and schools in the creation of Education Action Zones, the introduction of information technology, the promotion of lifelong learning and the reorganization of vocational education. It has become preoccupied with raising standards and seeking out the means to achieve this goal. Typically the direction is not through redistribution but through additional regulation and placing greater onus upon schools themselves, stressing leadership, good management and payment by results.

The 'joined-up' perspective (linking the work of functional agencies towards identifiable solutions) has become evidenced, for example, in the Sure Start programme designed to support families with young children in areas of poverty. This is aimed towards alleviation of health and social inequalities, and improvement of nursery education. Sure Start has its origins in the *Cross-Departmental Review of Provision for Young Children* (DfEE 1997), is targeted at disadvantaged areas and is concerned with improving the health and well-being of families and children before and after birth to maximize future educational opportunities for children. This includes support for parenting through reducing the impact of barriers stemming from different factors – social, economic, psychological, employment and housing. It is currently focused upon approximately one hundred 'trailblazer' sites around England. Sure Start is characteristic of New Labour's approach of providing substantive resourcing with the expectation of increased payment for productive results. The approach is to incentivize local discretion, to urge participation of local citizens and to define management based upon best partnership arrangements.

Modernizing the NHS – a distinct approach?

Modernization has become an umbrella term driving reform of health and social care. It applies to all parts of the care delivery process: organization, management and professional directions, client/patient inclusion. Adopting modern ideas and methods, the emphasis is on embracing improvements to standards and service quality. Modernization has been employed pragmatically by politicians to signify a process and an ideal of radical reform. It has been used as a term to describe a spectrum of changes and intended solutions. Its features include: openness; minimizing variations through national frameworks; flexibility and stripping out unnecessary (professional) demarcations; evidence-based practice; a philosophy of continuous improvement; partnership among provider agencies and service users; and challenging the status quo.

The modernization NHS Plan (DoH 2000) promised to put patients, not professionals, at the centre of the service. According to Ham (2000):

> To borrow the government's own vocabulary, the adoption of referral protocols and treatment guidelines offers a third way between a health service based on professionally defined need and one centred on untrammelled consumerism. If this trick can be brought off, then it will indeed be possible to offer more choice while achieving budgetary control.

Key principles of the Plan are to bolster the NHS as a public service; to meet public expectations more fully; to respond to different needs of different populations; to improve the quality of care; to provide a seamless service; to reduce health inequalities; and to provide open access to information. A central aim is to improve accountability locally through abolishing Community Health Councils (CHCs) and introducing citizens' panels (an independent local advisory panel in each health authority) and local authority scrutiny with the power to refer major service changes to the Secretary of State and nationally through increasing lay/ citizen membership of professional regulatory boards such as the United Kingdom Central Council for Nursing, Midwifery and Health Visiting (UKCC) and the General Medical Council (GMC), the NHS Modernization Board, an independent reconfiguration panel and the Commission for Health Improvement (CHImp); also there will be a Citizens' Council to advise the National Institute for Clinical Excellence (NICE). How to get patient organizations represented in the NHS is central to the Plan but it might legitimately be criticized for failing to lay out the kind of structure to engage broader communities in terms of representation and openness.

An essential focus of the modernization Plan is investment in staff and infrastructure: helping people to switch careers, modernizing pay structures and increasing earnings, and increasing throughput through training. The need for better workforce planning was identified in the earlier Tory reforms of health and community care but not actively progressed during the 1990s (Malin *et al.* 1999). Developing workforce capacity has now become central to the NHS Plan. A MORI poll conducted during September 2000 reported that staff shortages have overtaken pay as the main concern of nurses and that this was critical to giving high-quality patient care. Earlier, in February, the Health Secretary announced funding for the advanced training of new nurses and midwives, offering them a more responsible role in nursing (*The Times* 2000), as it had become recognized that they may leave the NHS because of bad pay, stress or being unable to manage their working hours around their children. Professional training leading to a joint qualification in nursing and social work is a further new development which has produced the 'joint practitioner' for services for people with learning disabilities (Davis *et al.* 1999).

Included in the Plan as a direct result of the March 2000 Budget settlement, it was stated that:

> The NHS will grow by one half in cash terms and by one third in real terms in just five years. More money will fund extra investment in NHS facilities: 7,000 extra beds in hospitals and intermediate care, over 100 new hospitals by 2010 and 500 new one-stop primary care centres, over 3,000 GP premises modernised and 250 new scanners . . . and investment in staff: 7,500 more consultants and 2,000 more GPs, 20,000 extra nurses and 6,500 extra therapists; 1,000 more medical school places and childcare support for NHS staff with 100 on-site nurseries.

Delivering services differently, as opposed to offering more of the same, is critical to reconciling rising demands and restricted budgets. Giving GPs direct access to hospital outpatient appointments and slots for day surgery, cutting bureaucratic delays and inefficiencies in waiting times for diagnosis and treatment, developing management of Care Trusts to commission health and social care within a single organization are core features of NHS Plan proposals.

Summary

The argument that the third way identifies a significantly different approach can probably be best evaluated by reference to policy implementation rather than through any theoretical insight it might offer. The claim on the one hand is that the third way approach argues in favour of reconstructing the state, and that the state should expand the role of the public sphere in the direction of transparency and openness. It should imply greater direct democracy and inclusivity. On the other hand, a pragmatic interpretation is that the third way entails a set of values to drive forward policy and to engender a sense of community and social responsibility.

Within New Labour's social policy agenda it has been viewed in terms of modernizing Old Labour strategies and/or merely an extension of neo-liberal, post-Thatcherite politics. On welfare policy reference has been made continuously to re-establishing links between rights and responsibilities, to ending welfare dependency and to deepening and widening citizen participation. Prominently, Giddens presents the third way as a response to five basic dilemmas including globalization, individualism and the perceived decadence of left–right politics. A prevailing perspective is one of lack of clarity over the general direction of New Labour's social policies, for example that of social exclusion and efforts to modernize health and social services provision. Basic structures remain unchanged; there is compliance with the market economy to deliver services yet added centralized regulation with the threat in extreme cases of state subjugation of local services if performance suggests a refusal to modernize.

The modernization programme for the NHS urges greater partnership, performance accountability and local discretion which is mirrored similarly within plans for education and social services provision. The general approach, described merely as a furtherance of managerialism within human services, represents an adaptation of earlier Conservative reforms but where standards can be raised through government fiat. The jury is still out over whether New Labour third way policies can effect radical change. It would seem that the approach is revisionist, idealistic in reforming aspirations, although rather embryonic in the sense of lacking robust foundation.

References

Beck, U. (1992) *Risk Society*. London: Sage.

Blair, T. (1998) *The Third Way*. London: Fabian Society.

Davis, A. (1999) A missed opportunity (White Paper Series Pt 3), *Community Care*, 18–24 March.

Davis, J., Rendell, P. and Sims, D. (1999) The joint practitioner – a new concept in professional training, *Journal of Interprofessional Care*, 3(4): 64–76.

DfEE (Department for Education and Employment) (1997) *Cross-Departmental Review of Provision for Young Children*. London: HMSO.

DoH (Department of Health) (1997) *The New National Health Service: Modern, Dependable*. London: HMSO.

DoH (Department of Health) (1998) *Modernising Social Services: Promoting Independence, Improving Protection, Raising Standards*. London: HMSO.

DoH (Department of Health) (2000) *The NHS Plan. A Plan for Investment, a Plan for Reform.* Cm 4818–1. London: HMSO.

Driver, S. and Martell, L. (1999) *New Labour: Politics after Thatcher.* Cambridge: Polity Press.

DSS (Department of Social Security) (1998) *A New Contract for Welfare: New Ambitions for our Country*, Cm 3805. London: The Stationery Office.

Etzioni, A. (1993) *The Spirit of Community: Rights, Responsibilities and the Communitarian Agenda.* London: Fontana Press.

Giddens, A. (1994) *Beyond Left and Right: The Future of Radical Politics.* Cambridge: Polity Press.

Giddens, A. (1998) *The Third Way.* Cambridge: Polity Press.

Ham, C. (2000) Going by the book, *The Guardian*, 29 September.

Hay, C. (1999) *The Political Economy of New Labour: Labouring under False Pretences?* Manchester: Manchester University Press.

Hutton, W. (1998) The price of a year's success, *The Observer*, 26 April.

Hutton, W. (1999) Blair in harmony: a new politics of values, *The Guardian*, 30 September.

Johnson, N. (1999) The personal social services and community care, in M. Powell (ed.) *New Labour, New Welfare State? The Third Way in British Social Policy.* Bristol: The Policy Press.

Labour Party (1996) *New Labour, New Life for Britain.* London: Labour Party.

Labour Party (1997) *New Labour, New Britain, Policy Guide*, General Election Edition. London: Labour Party.

Le Grand, J. (1982) *The Strategy of Equality.* London: George Allen and Unwin.

Le Grand, J. (1990) The State of Welfare, in J. Hills (ed.) *The State of Welfare.* Oxford: Clarendon Press.

Le Grand, J. (1998) The third way begins with CORA, *New Statesman*, 6 March: 26–7.

Malin, N., Manthorpe, J., Race, D. and Wilmot, S. (1999) *Community Care for Nurses and the Caring Professions.* Buckingham: Open University Press.

Miliband, D. (1994) From welfare to wealthfare, *Renewal*, Volume 2: 87–90.

Paton, C. (1999) New Labour's health policy: the new healthcare state, in M. Powell (ed.) *New Labour, New Welfare State? The Third Way in British Social Policy.* Bristol: The Policy Press.

Powell, M. (ed.) (1999) *New Labour, New Welfare State? The Third Way in British Social Policy.* Bristol: The Policy Press.

Snell, J. (1998) One day at a time (Mental Health), *Community Care*, 26 November–2 December.

Social Exclusion Unit (1998) *Bringing Britain Together: A National Strategy for Neighbourhood Renewal. Report by the Social Exclusion Unit.* Cm 4045. London: The Stationery Office.

The Times (2000) Shake-up will give nurses a bigger role, 29 February.

Wistow, G. (2000) Keeping the balance, *Community Care*, 31 August–6 September.

Wright, A. (1996) *Socialisms.* London: Routledge.

chapter two

IDENTIFYING THE HEALTH PROBLEM: NEED OR RISK?

Governments, welfare agencies, families and individuals all assess, manage and consider risk. This chapter discusses the relationship between social policy and risk. It does so because risk and its definitions or debates say much about what we understand to be the purposes and functions of social policies but also because risk is a fertile area in which to explore policy implementation, the role of values and the exercise of power. Risk relates to decision making on global or national scales but also at the level of personal and intimate behaviours. Risk and social policy therefore provide opportunities to debate and explore a number of themes already identified in this book and to make connections between them.

Defining and redefining risk

Despite its common currency, risk has a variety of definitions and usage. It is consistently used to represent danger or harm; indeed, Douglas (1990) has observed that 'the word risk now means danger; high risk means lots of danger' (p. 3). However, looking behind such 'self-evident' definitions are others which emphasize two important factors: probability or likelihood and outcome. Both merge into debates about risk and broaden its interpretation by raising elements of uncertainty and positive gains. In many ways, such word games are played out in the newspapers: front pages and 'news' debate the risks of war, pollution and disease. The back pages refer to sport and the risks of winning as well as losing, and the pleasure and pride of overcoming dangers. In between, the financial pages note the positive risks of calculating profit and gaining new business, or blame financial setbacks on inability to calculate risks correctly. Risk then is one of those words, like need and care, which raise a number of competing perspectives. Risk can be seen negatively and positively. It can evoke images of protection but also of empowerment. These competing perspectives are not simply between the lay or general public and professionals or experts. Risk is used in a variety of ways and for a variety of purposes.

Shaw and Shaw (2001) have traced the evolution of the term risk and the ways in which its positive and negative outcomes have changed in emphasis. They argue that the term has different characteristics that can be usefully considered through various social science perspectives. First, psychologists have emphasized the importance of risk perception and the need to understand how and why people make decisions about risk. Second, cultural theorists (or anthropologists) have identified social structures that lead to some problems being identified as risk issues and not others. Third, sociologists focus on the way social interests, power and access to social status affect how we perceive and manage risks. To illustrate this, we can take one 'social problem' which has been identified: the risk of teenage pregnancy. One approach is to explore young women's attitudes to 'risk taking' as part of their youth, their possible lack of assertiveness and their (mis)understanding of contraception. In cultural terms, their attitudes and behaviour may be linked or attributed to their image of themselves, their (low) ambitions and their views of alternatives. Sociological perspectives may alert us to the influences of class, social exclusion and unequal opportunities as well as reminding us that it is not only an issue affecting young women. All such perspectives about the risks of teenage pregnancy can be found in the report of the government's Social Exclusion Unit (1999) on the subject. While advocating a national campaign in order to tackle this social problem, groups at 'special risk' are identified (such as those in the care of local authorities) who need particular advice and support.

Risk, then, is used in policy statements and documents in a variety of ways. In the above example, the emphasis on probability or likelihood is high. Young women in the UK are defined as being at higher risk of pregnancy than their mainland European counterparts. Within this overall population, certain groups are at high risk or have a collection of 'risk factors' giving rise to concern. Government action is seen to be essential to reduce the rate of conception by addressing the multifaceted nature of the risk.

Such an approach to risk focuses on likelihood or chance factors, in addition to the outcome. But social policies have to concern themselves with outcomes: whether they are positive or negative. These can be highly contentious, since they may challenge deeply held values or beliefs. In the case of teenage pregnancy, for example, the Social Exclusion Unit

---

Box 2.1

Why teenage pregnancy matters
- There are higher rates in England than other European countries
- It affects disproportionately the poorest areas and most vulnerable young people
- Most young women who are sexually active wished they had not become sexually active so young
- Rates of conception and sexually transmitted disease are high among those not using contraception
- Abortion rates are high
- Relationships have a high chance of breakdown
- Links with poverty and unemployment are evident and can trap teenage parents
- Death, illness and accident rates among the babies and children of teenage mothers are higher than those of older mothers

Source: Social Exclusion Unit (1999)

---

constructs a lengthy set of arguments about why teenage pregnancy 'matters'. These set out the legitimacy for government interest in the generally private matters of sexuality and family life (see Box 2.1).

This debate, then, is about defining teenage pregnancy as a social problem: without overtly blaming either the young people or stigmatizing their children. The 'outcome' is a series of risks to the individual parent and child as well as negative social consequences. The policy debate has to establish that there is a legitimate role for government and that it is feasible for it to take action. These indicators are familiar in social policy analysis but have not generally been applied to risk. When outlining elements of intervention in areas of social policy, three main questions can be asked:

- Is this a legitimate area for government action?
- Is it possible that government can alter causes or contributory factors?
- Is it acceptable for government to take a role in this arena?

Such an analysis can be applied to other areas of public policy that focus on risk.

Risk as vulnerability

There are many uses of the word risk and a number of other terms have been clustered around the risk industry. These have been usefully

Figure 2.1 The risk iceberg
Source: Alaszewski (1998)

summarized by Alaszewski (1998) in a 'risk iceberg' (see Figure 2.1). As he observes, risk is associated with harm or danger, but on occasion with positive outcomes. Generally risk is what defines a dangerous person but it also can suggest that a person is vulnerable, in particular more vulnerable than others to experiencing harm or loss. The term 'vulnerable adults', for example, has recently been used by the Department of Health (DoH 2000a), in its guidance on local policies and procedures on the prevention of adult abuse. In this document, vulnerable adults are defined as 'at risk of abuse' (p. 6). They are those meeting the criteria of the NHS and Community Care Act 1990, or being in need of community care services by reason of mental or other disability, age or illness and being unable to take care of themselves or to protect themselves against 'significant harm or exploitation' (pp. 8–9).

While we may all be at risk – say, of crime – the term vulnerability is being used in such policies to stress the differences between people in terms of their ability to protect themselves. These differences are not fixed and a disability perspective would argue that casting disabled or older people, or people with health problems, as vulnerable is a form of infantilization and further perpetuates their less than full adult status. They can be seen as 'helpless' or 'dependent' and unable to manage the risks of ordinary living. Examples of this can be seen in the following snapshots:

- People with learning disabilities may be over-protected by those who fear they will be exploited, in particular sexually.
- Older people may be encouraged to move to residential care because it is too risky to live at home: it could be that with extra support they could manage to live in the community.

Box 2.2 Fright factors

Risks are more worrying and less acceptable if they are seen as

- Involuntary, e.g. pollution
- Inequitably distributed
- Inescapable
- Unfamiliar or new sources
- Man-made not natural causes
- Hidden and irreversible damage
- Possibly affecting more vulnerable groups such as children or pregnant women
- Resulting in a dreaded illness or form of death
- Creating identified victims
- Poorly understood by science
- Not understood or agreed by experts

Source: Calman *et al.* (1999)

- Young people leaving local authority care may have been poorly equipped with the skills of ordinary living to manage independent living: some may move from crisis to crisis and be seen as unable to function without paternalistic control.

Stereotypes of 'client groups' often suggest that people with disabilities, or those who are very young or very old, are less able to evaluate the risks of ordinary life. This may be unfair since most of us make guesses about the likelihood of harm or danger. Some risks are overestimated, particularly those which frighten people because they are involuntary, novel, man-made and inescapable (Calman *et al.* 1999). These 'fright factors' are set out in Box 2.2 and can help to explain high levels of public concern about terrorist activities and diseases such as new variant CJD (Creutzfeldt-Jacob disease). In the aftermath of the terrorist attacks in the United States on 11 September 2001, for example, many Americans chose to travel by car instead of aeroplane despite the greater risk of car accidents.

In the UK, nv CJD is an example of such a risk evoking particular fear. It appears to be linked to new developments in farming and the food industry – both poorly understood by the public. It also appears beyond the control of ordinary families who trusted experts in safety and in disease communication. Like bovine spongiform encephalopathy (BSE) or AIDS, it has been poorly understood and subject to contradictory advice. Victims and their tragic stories evoke particular sympathy.

> **Box 2.3**
>
> Social capital includes 'features of social organisation, such as networks, norms and trust, that facilitate co-ordination and co-operation for mutual benefit' (Putnam 1995: 67)

Trust and risk

The reaction of public policy to risk is on several levels. Key to reducing risk or the fear of risk is the extent to which the state or government is trusted to act in the best interests of its citizens. Similarly, trust in experts is one element of countering alarm over risk. Theories of social capital (for example, see Putnam 1995) also indicate that trust between citizens in communities can act as a form of social 'glue' which can provide stability and a sense of mutual support and its practical expression (see Box 2.3).

Social capital is perhaps the other end of the spectrum from what is often referred to as the 'risk society' (Beck 1992). This term has become commonplace in pointing to a 'runaway world' (Giddens 2000) in which major forces such as globalization and the movement of people and capital create a rapid, ever-changing and somehow smaller world. Giddens (2000) has distinguished between two types of risk. The first, *external risk*, is that arising from tradition or nature. *Manufactured risk* is a second form and has been created by the processes of modernization. For him, there is a turning point in which societies move from concern about external risks, such as floods or plague, to recognizing that disasters and accidents or freaks of nature may be caused by human actions, for example, global warming or the spread of infectious diseases. At such a time 'we start worrying less about what nature can do to us, and more about what we have done to nature' (Giddens 2000). Trust in politicians is fractured, with widespread belief that they may be scaremongering or involved in cover-ups. A 'risk society' presents a challenge to social policy making and implementation at local and even national level. Problems of movements of distressed people around the world as refugees and asylum seekers cannot be addressed by national controls. Even policies central to family life, such as the care and protection of children, are now affected by problems such as child abduction, international paedophile rings and the cross-country electronic trafficking of pornography. Both debates over social capital and the broader discussions of a risk society often see individuals as homogeneous. Risk, however, is not equally distributed and may affect certain groups, communities or individuals disproportionately. Risk can give rise to conflict: for the protection of some individuals may leave others more vulnerable. Driving children to school, or young people to a party, may protect these children, but extra volumes of traffic present risks to other children as pedestrians or cyclists. Part of policy making is a balance of risks and a discussion of how to evaluate the impact of decision making. This occurs at all levels of government, central and local, and within other decision-making bodies: whether these are schools, voluntary groups or self-help community activities.

Risk decision making is a process of assessing risks and acknowledging that knowledge is often patchy and imperfect. It is often based on a 'snapshot' in time and research can be limited or has to be 'borrowed' from other arenas. Professionals are trusted as experts in a particular field of knowledge as people who are better equipped than the general public to make such decisions. They have received training, they have been judged as capable or competent and they accumulate experience. However, in managing risk rather than certainties, professionals will make the wrong decision at times. A series of tragedies in the 1990s, in particular, have resulted in a series of high-profile inquiries in the UK which have allowed us to see more of the world of professional decision making and the management of risk. Their findings have influenced policy, notably in mental health but also in the area of inspection and regulation of social and health care and in respect of professional regulation. Findings from the inquiries often report that risk assessment should be given greater priority, although many practitioners have seen this as a call for greater accountability and defensive practice, rather than improving services for and communication with people with mental health problems (Stanley and Manthorpe 2001). In response, the government has made piecemeal changes to mental health legislation and a commitment to reforming mental health law to reflect priority of risk.

All assessment, however, whether it is in respect of the care and treatment of an individual or a set of policies, is part of decision making. The processes can also be referred to as policy appraisal, where similar calculations of costs and benefits are discussed. In some areas, decision-making 'tools' are developed, allowing people to set out the framework for their discussion and choices. Four examples of this process come from different areas: child protection, environmental impacts, new genetics and accidents.

Decision making: example one – child protection

The issue of child protection combines what are known as 'wicked issues', central to social policy, with the uncertainties of risk. As Munro observes, 'Childhood deaths from parental abuse have become a symbol of tragic waste and an outcome that our sophisticated welfare services should be able to prevent' (1999: 117). However, she warns that this preoccupation with risk has meant that professionals overestimate the risk of abuse since the consequences of 'getting it wrong' are so danger- ous, both to children and to professionals themselves. Such overestim- ates mean that social workers, or other members of the caring professions, for example nurses or doctors, may be regarded as intervening or inter- fering in the private world of the family. Professionals are under pressure 'to avoid mistakes of any kind' (Munro 1999: 119). Not only does this alter the relationships of the professionals with families, making it hard for families to see professionals as supportive, it also means that much of social services expenditure and attention is directed at those cases of possible child abuse. It is of course impossible to predict with certainty which child will be abused and which will not. Munro has identified the problem of false positives – families being wrongly considered to be abusive – and false negatives, when abusive families are not identified (p. 123). When politicians or the public are very concerned, possibly in the wake of a tragic child death or in the aftermath of a public inquiry, the number of false positives may rise.

Munro argues that there are lessons for public policy from this focus on child protection. It is important for public education to convey the idea that risk assessment is never certain and that the public (and politi- cians) need to recognize that it is not possible to identify all children in danger. Similarly, much social policy, as this book has argued, involves values. Risk is not a simple matter of calculating the probability of harms or benefits. It is about values, and some of these may be competing, such as the privacy of family life set against the rights of children to protec- tion. Smacking a child, for example, can be seen as mistreatment but it is a social and political decision as to whether such an action is classified as abuse, or as a matter with which the state should concern itself. Values help us to make such decisions.

Linked to values and also to other themes that arise when considering risk is the notion of blame or scapegoating. It can be easy to 'demonize' parents, rather than thinking about supporting parents in difficult cir- cumstances or under particular stresses. If poverty and unemployment are risk factors for social problems, then it may make more sense and require more expense to consider issues of social exclusion.

Finally, as Munro argues, child protection provides an illustration of risk in that it is difficult to identify a place of safety for a child, once he or she has been removed from the family. All alternatives have their risks as another catalogue of inquiries into residential child care abuses has demonstrated (see Stanley *et al.* 1999). The illusory search for 'safe options' in public policy may raise public expectations only to disappoint them and cause a loss of trust in experts or allegations of cover-up.

Decision making: example two – environmental policy

Including the environment in a discussion of risk makes sense because issues such as global warming, nuclear accidents and pollution figure strongly in illustrations of the risk society. In 1991, the UK government noted that many of its civil servants were involved in policies that affected and were affected by the environment (DoE 1991). Linked to this is growing appreciation that social policies are rarely discrete to one region or country but cross nations and continents. Deacon (1998) has described this 'shrinking world' and the importance of understanding the roles of international organizations such as the World Bank and International Labour Office, and the World Trade Organization. He argues that there are crucial issues such as the extent to which the World Bank and the International Monetary Fund are accountable, and to whom. Against this can be set the power of citizens to defend their own interests and rights by use of international courts and agreements. In the UK, the recent introduction of the Human Rights Act 1998 is beginning to impact upon debates about individual rights, and is evidence of how European citizens' rights may be converging.

Within this complicated framework, policy making must therefore reflect local and national concerns but also the wider international arena. Environmental policy can thus range 'from street-corner to stratosphere' (DoE 1991). One way of establishing policy options is to set them out in a form of appraisal. This can assist in clarifying the objectives of policy and also in ensuring that the various options have all been identified and explored. Box 2.4 sets out the step-by-step approach to policy appraisal identified by the Department of the Environment (DoE 1991).

This is a systematic approach, which sets out a decision-making process. In the real world many factors may influence this rational approach. Some options will conflict with other policies or values, some decisions may be tied to others and so on. But such an approach does allow for a broad range of views, particularly if information from 'experts' is taken to include a range of stakeholders, not just scientists or academic commentators. It also allows for a broad interpretation of 'costs and benefits' so that these are not just seen in immediate or financial terms.

Decision making: example three – new genetics

Genetic research evokes high levels of anxiety but also high levels of anticipation. National governments may find that their own attempts to make policy in this area are leapfrogged by international developments. The promise of cures for illnesses and the solution to difficulties such as

---

Box 2.4

The steps of policy appraisal

- A summary of the issue – using expert sources to build knowledge
- Identifying the objectives – putting them into priority
- Assessing any constraints – how many, what strength
- Thinking through the options – as wide a range as possible, including doing nothing
- Identifying the costs and benefits
- Weighing up the costs and benefits
- Exploring the options – what might be factors affecting them
- Choosing a preferred option – and explaining the choice
- Setting up a monitoring system
- Evaluating the policy

Source: DoE (1991: 2)

---

infertility make the issue of genetics of relevance to current and future generations. For policy makers, 'new genetics', an area involving a range of research arising from studies of the human genome, requires attention to debates where scientific expertise is required but where public expectations are multifaceted and major commercial interests are at stake.

Fitzpatrick (2001) has argued that eugenics has had a weak direct influence on British welfare policy but indirectly it is possible to trace influences on health promotion, maternal well-being and attitudes and practices related to birth control and reproduction. However, in the twenty-first century he proposes that biotechnology, a scientific successor to some eugenic theories and practices, needs to be regulated rather than left unmonitored. One element of such regulation is highly relevant to risk: it is the precautionary principle that asserts that in conditions of uncertainty a low-risk, 'conservative' approach is necessary.

Fitzpatrick applies principles of welfare, equality and liberty (in other words, values) to examples of practices that occasionally make general news but may affect families and individuals directly. Genetic screening, for example, can have social and individual benefits; we may wish to know if we have a high chance of a genetic disorder or likelihood of contracting a disease. However, if we have a family history of a disease we may not wish to know this, may not want to be excluded from a job or mortgage or denied insurance because of this enhanced risk.

Genetic screening, however, is not simply a matter of balancing the interests of those with enhanced risks against the desires or interests of those at no risk or low risk who may desire reduced insurance premiums. Genetic screening itself can cause harm:

False positives needlessly generate anxiety; false negatives reassure even though something may really be wrong, and remove the possibility of helpful interventions, leading to resentment when the mistake is finally discovered.

(Chadwick 1999: 295)

Furthermore, finding that you are at low risk of disease may mean that you take it as a certainty or continue an unhealthy lifestyle.

Debates about genetic screening tend to see individuals as rational and autonomous with the ability to make choices and appreciate the consequences. This view of individual agency has been recently stressed as important in debates about social policy in contrast to views which saw individuals as powerless in the face of economic and social forces (see Le Grand 1997). There is now more attention to the way individuals interact with welfare systems and how they may ignore, alter or subvert official strictures or guidance. Making decisions about risk, for example, is one way in which individuals may behave very differently according to their own values or preferences. Health is an area where such behaviours may occur with people choosing 'risky behaviour' in the face of evidence or professional advice. This may apply in respect of vaccination, diet or healthy lifestyles. Some writers have argued that such risk decisions impinge on key responsibilities for family health and well-being. Lippman (1999), for example, says that women's rights to choose are now being viewed as narrow and individualized. She argues that the choices on offer centre on biomedical interventions, such as screening, testing and medication. Women may feel 'worse off' if they refuse offers for testing and blamed if they do not take up options that they may think risky or discriminatory. Lippman asks, for example, 'Can I say no when asked if I want prenatal diagnosis without being made to feel culpable if I refuse testing and a baby with Down's syndrome is born?' (p. 287). She notes that such tests are part of a concentration on prevention and avoidance but that less priority seems to be given to the support of families with disabled children.

Genetic screening presents a new challenge to social policy. An understanding of risk helps us to see that values are important, that there are negative as well as positive outcomes to such developments and that expert views will not prevail unless there is a degree of trust in the advice given and some respect of uncertainty and precautionary principles. In the UK, the Human Genetics Advisory Commission and the Human Fertilisation and Embryology Authority have become important political structures to develop advice for policy makers and to promote trust among the public by bringing together scientific, lay and ethical perspectives, at a distance from policy implementation and commercial interests (see websites: HGAC and HFEA).

Decision making: example four – the risk of accidents

As a subject of social policy, accidents do not figure highly in discussion or writings. But much social policy is concerned with what might, in previous times or in other cultures, be termed accidents. Classic characteristics of accidents seem to revolve around notions that they are random, unpredictable, inevitable and blame-free occurrences (see Green 1997). As a form of social insurance, spreading and sharing risks between individuals and various groups in society, the post-war welfare state can be viewed as a means of providing some assurance that accidents of injury, ill health or sheer bad luck (widowhood, being orphaned, having an 'accident') will have some elements of their harm minimized.

Green argues that interpretations of accidents have changed so that almost any 'accidental' event can be interpreted as someone's or something's fault, or at least to have a cause that can be identified through a process of investigation or inquiry. Death, for example, is no accident but the result of disease or injury. Green observes that such interpretations tend to be made in a society where the impact of negative events can be calculated and ameliorated by insurance. National insurance and the payment of welfare benefits is one example, in the case of younger widows (and widowers). Increasingly, she argues, we are personally responsible for reducing the risk of accidents and making arrangements to manage them if they arise. It is our responsibility to wear crash helmets and seat belts, to obey the Highway Code and to behave as responsible pedestrians. It is our responsibility to safeguard our possessions and our children. To some extent the state has moved increasingly into such areas: it is the law in the UK that ensures helmets are worn almost universally on motorcycles and seat belts are generally adopted. At a more general level, traffic itself is highly regulated and monitored. Within the home, a variety of health and safety guidelines and requirements on manufacturers exist to minimize the risk of accidents. In the workplace, the powers of the Health and Safety Executive have continued to regulate the dangers of the work environment, with inspections, advice and enforcement powers.

Accidents, however, remain a major source of social distress, no matter how they are reclassified as non-accidental. One key finding relevant to social exclusion debates and the health of the nation is that accidents are not randomly distributed among the population. Roberts and her colleagues (1992) found that 'the steep social class gradient for accidents in the United Kingdom (which is steeper, even, than the socio-economic gradient for ill-health overall) has frequently been documented, but remains poorly explained . . .'. They investigated this issue by focusing on a housing estate in Glasgow where there was said to be a high rate of childhood accidents. Doing this they chose to explore the incidence and prevalence of such accidents by looking at the data but they also asked families living on the estate about their own perceptions of the risks of accidents. Such an approach takes a 'bottom-up' view to social problems implementation (see Sabatier 1986), a perspective which argues that it is important to consider how policy is mediated and changed as it moves from formal and legal levels to operate in the real and complex world.

Roberts and her colleagues suggested that the high level of accidents could be interpreted in a variety of ways. It could be, for example:

- that the children behaved dangerously;
- that their parents provided inadequate supervision;
- that families did not know about the risks of the estate;
- that families lacked resources to provide safety equipment or to divert their children from dangerous activities.

In their observations and discussions, Roberts and her colleagues found that the children were at risk from the dangers present on the estate, such as lack of play space, and that parents were aware of this. However, the alternatives were also seen as 'risky': parents feared sending their children to the park, for example. Such perceptions place accidents in the context of a wider environment of insecurity in which 'strangers' and places which might once have been thought 'safe' are increasingly viewed as risky. The researchers considered that child safety is as much about environment as behaviour. They found parents were aware of the risks to their children but had to balance risks against each other – the risk of playing outside near home, or going out of sight and out of contact. Parents prioritize certain dangers or risks over others and child-ren themselves manage risks. However, in an environment of dangers, both parents and children may only have limited room to manoeuvre. Rather than giving insensitive or dogmatic instruction, possibly alienating families or causing them further anxiety, experts or professionals may have a role in promoting collective responsibility and environ-mental improvement.

Conclusion

Developing public policy around risk sets a new range of challenges for politicians and advisory communities. The four areas discussed above indicate the chorus of demands for protection and certainty coupled with desires for choice and personal freedoms. Trust is a concept which government has seen as helping to promote confidence and quality of service delivery. The NHS itself is committed to being a 'high-trust' organization (DoH 2000b: para. 6.1). Whether government and organizations like the NHS trust members of the public is less evident from policy documents.

References

Alaszewski, A. (1998) Risk in modern society, in A. Alaszewski, L. Harrison and J. Manthorpe (eds) *Risk, Health and Welfare*. Buckingham: Open University Press.

Beck, U. (1992) *Risk Society: Towards a New Modernity*. Sage: London.

Calman, K. C., Bennett, P. G. and Coles, D. G. (1999) Risks to health: some key issues in management regulation and communication, *Health, Risk and Society*, 1(1): 107–16.

Chadwick, R. (1999) Genetics, choice and responsibility, *Health, Risk and Society*, 1(3): 293 300.

Deacon, B. (1998) Social policy in a shrinking world, in P. Alcock, A. Erskine and M. May (eds) *The Student's Companion to Social Policy*. Oxford: Blackwell.

DoE (Department of the Environment) (1991) *Policy Appraisal and the Environment*. London: HMSO.

DoH (Department of Health) (2000a) *No Secrets: Guidance on Developing and Implementing Multi-agency Policies and Procedures to Protect Vulnerable Adults from Abuse*. London: Department of Health.

DoH (Department of Health) (2000b) *The NHS Plan*. A Plan for Investment, a Plan for Reform, Cm 4818–1. London: The Stationery Office.

Douglas, M. (1990) *Risk Acceptability According to the Social Sciences*. London: Routledge and Kegan Paul.

Fitzpatrick, T. (2001) Before the cradle: new genetics, biopolicy and regulated eugenics, *Journal of Social Policy*, 30(4): 589–612.

Giddens, A. (2000) *Runaway World: How Globalization is Reshaping Our Lives*. London: Routledge.

Green, J. (1997) *Risk and Misfortune: The Social Construction of Accidents*. London: University College London Press.

Le Grand, J. (1997) Knights, knaves or pawns? Human behaviour and social policy, *Journal of Social Policy*, 26(2): 149–69.

Lippman, A. (1999) Choice as a risk to women's health, *Health, Risk and Society*, 1(3): 281–92.

Munro, E. (1999) Protecting children in an anxious society, *Health, Risk and Society*, 1(1): 117–27.

Putnam, R. (1995) Bowling alone: America's declining social capital, *Journal of Democracy*, 6: 65–78.

Roberts, H., Smith, S. and Lloyd, M. (1992) Safety as social value: a community approach, in S. Scott, G. Williams, S. Platt and H. Thomas (eds) *Private Risks and Public Dangers*. Aldershot: Avebury.

Sabatier, P. A. (1986) Top-down and bottom-up approaches to implementation research: a critical analysis and suggested synthesis, *Journal of Public Policy*, 21–48.

Shaw, A. and Shaw, I. (2001) Risk research in a risk society, *Research Policy and Planning*, 19(1): 3–16.

Social Exclusion Unit (1999) *Teenage Pregnancy*, Cm 4342. London: The Stationery Office.

Stanley, N. and Manthorpe, J. (2001) Reading mental health inquiries: messages for social work, *Journal of Social Work*, 1(1): 77–99

Stanley, N., Manthorpe, J. and Penhale, B. (eds) (1999) *Institutional Abuse: Perspectives Across the Life Course*. London: Routledge.

chapter **three**

RESPONSIBILITY AND SOLIDARITY

Introduction

The focus of this chapter is the relationship between the principles of individual responsibility and social solidarity. I shall begin by briefly defining these concepts as I intend to use them.

The principle of individual responsibility concerns the power of individuals over their own actions, and their answerability for those actions. It rests on a concept of individual agency which owes much to the eighteenth-century philosopher Immanuel Kant, and which continues to influence modern liberalism. For Kant individual agency and rationality were inextricably linked, and even though an individual might choose to act irrationally, the option of using reason had to be available to that individual for them to be an agent in the first place. In ethical terms the appropriate guide for agency in Kant's view is reason. To identify one's moral duty one must apply reason. The principle of social solidarity is rooted in a view that individuals have obligations toward their fellow human beings going beyond the basic responsibility of respecting their liberty, and extending into mutual assistance and support.

The tension between these principles is identifiable in the development of social and health care in the past twenty-five years. It is particularly evident that the Conservative government elected in 1979 sought during its eighteen years in office to enhance the importance of individual responsibility as a guiding principle in its policy, and that the Labour government elected in 1997, while retaining a degree of commitment to individual responsibility, has sought to balance it with a greater emphasis on social solidarity. But before we explore the implications of these principles as influences on recent social and health care, we need to reflect further on their meaning in historical terms. In order to do that I propose first to consider the significance of a major change in our understanding of the individual since the nineteenth century.

The individual and the collective

The idea of the individual, developing through protestantism and liberalism, is predicated on the proposition that we can most usefully understand human beings by considering 'the individual' as the paradigm of humanity. Lukes (1973) in his discussion of the concept of individualism identifies as a central tenet that the individual is fundamental, while society is contingent. He also adds to the concept of the individual the moral characteristics of dignity, autonomy, privacy and self-development. For the individualist, the actions and decisions of individuals taken in aggregate guide us in our understanding of society. For instance, Mill (1962) viewed society as moulded by the efforts of the individuals within it to maximize their own happiness. So our understanding of the individual enables us to understand society.

Within this conceptual framework, the characteristics that make individuals the most valid and fundamental version of human-ness must include the ability to take moral responsibility for their actions. Anything that compromises responsibility compromises individuality. Solidarity can also be understood in these terms. Respect for the individual implies mutual respect between individuals, since what is to be respected about the individual is to be respected in every individual. And solidarity for a commentator such as Rorty (1994) is a relationship freely entered into within a community of autonomous individuals, and thereby a valid expression of individual autonomy.

Individualism is countered by a collectivist view that human beings can only be properly understood as part of a collectivity – a community or society. Marxism has given a particularly powerful account of the degree to which each human being's behaviour and identity are products of collective features from economy through culture to consciousness. In this view, to see the individual in isolation is to miss the main features of the human being. One of the major criticisms of the concept of the individual agent as defined by Kant is that it is too far removed from our understanding of human beings to be helpful, and in particular seems bereft of social location, without culture, without affiliations, loyalties or social identity. Gray (1995: 50) comments that 'The conception of ourselves as autonomous rational agents and authors of our own values bears patently upon it the marks of modernity and European individuality and has no universality as an image of moral life'. Collectivist perspectives place limits on the range of individual responsibility, as they argue that people cannot be held fully responsible for actions which are constrained by influences beyond their control. Also, collectivism offers a model of solidarity rather different from the individualist model in both a practical and a moral sense; a view that actions, experiences and opportunities are primarily interdependent, and that the responsibility for such decisions should be shared, as the effects are shared.

Historical background

Individualism was dominant in Western Europe and North America in the late eighteenth and nineteenth centuries, both in culture and in state policy. The development of the view of the individual as a rational autonomous agent, elaborated in important ways by Kant, is a significant part of the development of liberalism over that period, and is closely linked to the development of capitalism. In fact it has deeper roots, in the puritan of the seventeenth century, for whom the virtues of the godly and those of the prosperous coincided. As Tawney (1990: 249) pointed out, the virtues of the puritan were 'intensity and earnestness of labour, concentration, system and method, the initiative which broke with routine and the foresight which postponed the present to the future'. As puritanism's successor, eighteenth- and nineteenth-century liberalism viewed the individual agent in the context of a competitive capitalist economy, requiring of the individual an ability to take risks and adhere to rules. Both of these required a high degree of rationality and self-discipline. Where ill-judged actions could result in ruin, a stark and disciplined sense of the weightiness of one's decisions was a crucial part of the moral and social repertoire of the middle-class male. Agency in that sense was highly instrumental, in that actions were closely associated with the preserving or losing of prosperity or even life.

The development of an oppositional analysis of nineteenth-century capitalism, particularly through Marxism, provided a counterbalance to this individualistic perspective. The demands of politics and war during the early twentieth century also gave a fillip to a more collective view (Cronin 1991) and the subsequent decades of social change created a very different economy of consequences for the individual agent from those prevailing in the eighteenth and nineteenth centuries. Economic development transformed the individual's prospects of material comfort and material security in such a way that the threats represented by material loss, poverty and homelessness were somewhat reduced. Materially most western societies became safer in the twentieth century, and this provided a cushion against the worst consequences of unwise or unfortunate decisions. Political development allowed a part of that material prosperity to be appropriated by government to provide the safety net of the welfare state, seeking to reduce further the material risks of living.

These developments were accompanied by cultural changes which are central to the focus of this chapter. These changes have involved a number of elements. First, following the development of Freudian psychology there was a shift in the perceived centre of power in individual motivation, from the rational to the irrational, and from choice to causation. Individuals increasingly came to be seen as partly controlled by unconscious forces for which they cannot be held fully responsible. Second, following from changes in political and social thinking there was a greater predisposition to see individual behaviour as being determined by collective factors. In the middle period of the twentieth century, when these developments could be seen near their high water mark, the contemporary philosopher Mabbott, looking back over the previous hundred years, commented that 'from that time [1850] onward, Darwin in Biology, Marx in Sociology, Pavlov and Freud in Psychology, were advancing causal explanations across the frontiers of life and mind' (Mabbott 1966: 110).

Recent developments

However, these trends have been countered in recent decades. Economic security has been challenged by the problems of western economies since the oil crisis of 1973. Collectivism has lost ground somewhat in the past twenty-five years, having come under attack from commentators of the renascent right, and having been explicitly rejected by the 1979 Conservative government (George and Wilding 1985). The 1997 Labour government has restored some limited legitimacy to collectivist ideas, but they have not regained their earlier currency. Over the same period deterministic psychological perspectives were rejected by writers such as Capra (1984) in favour of humanistic and cognitive models of psychology which emphasized free will and choice; and collectivist social perspectives lost credibility by the discrediting of Marxism. This is not to say that the cultural effects of the first half of the twentieth century have been simply reversed by the reactions of the last quarter-century. For instance, Gray (1997: 3) argues that the neo-liberal project of Thatcherism proved a 'self-limiting project' that failed to produce the cultural change necessary to legitimize unfettered market economics. There is ample evidence, for example, that the British population have retained throughout the Conservative years a deep attachment to the NHS (Hutton 2000). So there has not been a cultural reversion to nineteenth-century individualism. But that is not to say that important cultural developments have not occurred.

The development of consumer culture is a major part of this. It was already well developed in the 1960s and 1970s, but the growth in the consumer economy in the past twenty-five years has increased its impact. The experience of the consumer is in one sense an experience of autonomy and agency, but the nature of that autonomy is open to question. Lee (1993) argues that modern consumerism is fuelled by a constructed desire for goods with symbolic value, rather than the rational desire for goods with practical use which fuelled earlier capitalism. The gratification of those constructed desires is itself something that the consumer is dependent on the producer and advertiser to achieve. It is therefore difficult for consumers to establish independently whether they have achieved their desires, and more difficult to know what that achievement – that gratification – might feel like. Material success in the production-oriented capitalist society of the nineteenth century could readily be measured in monetary terms, and the citizen could make a rational judgement as to what he or she was 'worth'. In Lee's view the contemporary consumer cannot do this, and some of the 'territory' accessible to rational judgement is lost to the individual, who is open to manipulation at a non-rational level in the consumer market. Habermas (1996) also argues that hedonistic irrationality is a direct product of the successful colonization of culture by modern consumer capitalism.

While the consumer role has increased in importance, change in the deployment of labour has steadily reduced the average citizen's direct contact with the process of material production closely associated with nineteenth-century capitalism. The post-1970s reassertion of business practices associated with neo-liberal economics has further disconnected people from the productive side of economic activity, through greater job insecurity, creating further marginalization from productive processes described vividly by Sennett (1998) in the US. As Sennett points out, this retreat of secure employment has also removed a major yardstick through which individuals can make a rational and independent judgement of their own social worth and importance.

Agency

The result of all this is that the experience of agency has changed, moving from what could be termed the instrumental agency of the eighteenth- and nineteenth-century bourgeois to something that might be called expressive agency – agency which is less focused on creating and distributing the output necessary to survive and prosper within an economic system, and more focused on experiencing and enjoying social and personal living. This connects with Giddens's argument (Giddens 1991) that the output of this mode of experiencing life is a constantly revised self, expressed through changing and evolving lifestyle choices. Expressive agents in their personal living are consumers rather than producers of their social world, and decisions are geared to self-expression and enjoyment. This is not to say that most people are not instrumental agents as well. Clearly there are decisions required of most citizens on which future viability and even survival can still depend. But the experience of expressive agency dominates.

This change has implications for our views of both responsibility and solidarity. The principle of responsibility depends upon the existence of the rational agent, and it is therefore affected by this shift in agency. Agents who are manipulated through the mechanisms of consumer society must be seen as having their agency somewhat compromised. But solidarity is also affected, though in a more subtle way. The rationalist idea of solidarity as a human bond depends on the enlightenment view of persons, in particular on Kant's view of persons as ends in themselves, providing the shared basis for a morality of mutual respect (Paton 1978). The rationality of the person is the basis of the status that persons are therefore duty-bound to ascribe to one another. The ability to hold one another responsible for our actions is a fundamental requirement of solidarity.

Policy and politics

The development of policy in relation to health and social care over the past two decades has interacted closely with the ideas which I have outlined. I propose to discuss these developments, which I shall then relate to the function and position of three key social institutions – the state, the family and the community as foci of policy and as contexts of social solidarity and individual responsibility. I should add that a fourth institution, the market, also plays a part in this narrative, but as it is considered in more depth in another chapter, it will receive more cursory treatment here.

In the 1970s commentators of the New Right argued that British society had undergone a real behavioural change in the post-war years that had negative social and economic consequences. People were becoming less willing to engage in wealth-creating activities – working hard, setting up in business – and these were becoming unfashionable aspirations. The New Right blamed this on the increasing involvement of the state in the economy and society, cushioning individuals against the penalties of indolence and incompetence, and preventing them from gaining the rewards of industry, enterprise and thrift. People were also becoming less willing to make the commitments and sacrifices necessary to create families and rear children properly. Parents were less willing to stay together for the duration of a childrearing period, and less willing to make the effort involved in moulding the behaviour of their children in a socially acceptable direction. This was blamed on a culture of mixed indulgence and interference, again arising from an over-generous but interfering state, which sapped the will of the citizen to take responsibility for family life. This view was expressed particularly strongly by Dennis (1993). In the terminology of this discussion, right-wing commentators were seeing a retreat from instrumental agency, to the detriment of society and economy.

When the Thatcher government came to power in 1979, it sought to respond to all these concerns. The essential thrust of its policy was to move the state away from the social democratic shape it had taken over the previous four decades and toward the liberal model, by reducing state involvement in the economy, reducing the welfare state and increasing the range of areas where individuals make their own decisions about their welfare provision (Edgell and Duke 1991). Pressure was applied to people in various ways to push them back toward greater self-sufficiency and less dependence on the state. Health and social care constituted an important and challenging arena for the application of New Right principles.

Thatcherism and health

In 1979 the National Health Service seemed to be a perfect example of uncontrolled state expenditure. The period from 1974 had been characterized by increasing anxiety about the rising cost of the NHS and the difficulties of controlling it. Attempts at planning after 1974 were patchy in their success, and the new government in 1979 perceived it as still costly and inefficient. It was also seen as inimical to individual responsibility through its fostering of a culture of waste and complacency among its employees, and of dependence and passivity among the population, as well as being bereft of the market virtues of producer and consumer. Certainly it could be argued that the delivery of health care in the NHS fostered, and still fosters, passivity among those on the receiving end. There is ample evidence that the patient experience is one of relative passivity and disempowerment (see for instance Taylor and Field 1993), though the main causes of this may well be the processes through which state health care is delivered, rather than the fact of state health care in itself. Methods of health care delivery tend to enhance dependency, and the status of the medical profession in relation to most patients adds to this dependency a degree of social disempowerment. Before 1990 the main components of the NHS were in the 'producer' role in terms of health care production, and the system was thus producer-dominated.

The patient as 'consumer' had very little power. So for those who had direct experience of the patient role, the experience was likely not to be conducive to an enhanced degree of individual responsibility. Having said all this, it is probably fair to say that, for the same reasons, the patient experience in the NHS was also not conducive to solidarity. The power of the medical profession and the patient experience of powerlessness, in relation to both access to treatment (particularly the waiting list experience) and to the nature of treatment, is likely to foster alienation rather than solidarity. But that is not to say that the NHS as a whole was or is inimical to solidarity. It was clearly an expression of solidarity in its creation, and the fact that the population remains deeply attached to it (see Hutton 2000) suggests that to some degree it remains so. However, this was not of concern to the government in 1979. They were primarily concerned with promoting individual responsibility, and their policies were geared to this.

This goal was pursued in three ways. First, attempts were made to limit the proportion of national wealth which the NHS consumed. This was pursued through attempts to increase efficiency – notably through the introduction of general management. In some respects this continued the process initiated in 1974 and constituted a real attempt to change the culture of the NHS. However, these problems were addressed in a more fundamental way by the introduction of the internal market in 1990. This shifted the centre of gravity of policy from reliance on managers to keep costs down on the basis of directives, to the creation of incentives to maximize efficiency through the internal market. However, there was no direct role available for the patient in the internal market. Market discipline was aimed at the doctors and managers rather than patients and, although it shifted the producer-dominated culture of the previous NHS, the countervailing force was 'purchasers' (health authorities and fundholding GPs), not the patient. It is clear that the main motive of this reform was efficiency, rather than social engineering. The individual patient was no more individually responsible than before the changes.

However, another strategy was also being pursued which addressed the patient-as-citizen more directly. During the 1980s and 1990s health promotion policy was articulated through two major statements – *Promoting Better Health* (DoH 1987) and *The Health of the Nation* (DoH 1992). This strand of policy sought to reduce the importance of the NHS as an illness service and attempted instead to focus on prevention. This led into an area of major ideological importance for the Thatcherite project – the location of responsibility for health with the individual. In these and related policy documents collective factors affecting health – environmental and social factors such as social class differences, the impact of pollution – were largely ignored and health was presented as the responsibility of individuals and their lifestyle decisions. It is this area where the patient-citizen has been encouraged into the consumer role, as health conciousness and healthy living has become a lifestyle option with considerable potential for commodification. This policy fitted well with some of the cultural changes discussed above, and both political and cultural factors can be seen as contributing during this time to the development of a health market and a health industry focusing on lifestyle choices combining psychological, somatic and cosmetic issues. As Bunton and Burrows point out, 'under late modernity the dominant culture is one in which health, self identity and consumption are closely intertwined' (1995: 207). They also argue that the modern self-identity 'in turn demands of the self and the body greater "plasticity" which can only be achieved by the subtle calculation of appropriate patterns of consumption akin to those expounded by health promotion' (1995: 208). Here we can perhaps see an example of the process of self-creation described by Giddens. It is also arguably an example of how an activity which might be seen as a focus of instrumental agency (health and survival) has in fact become a focus for expressive agency.

Thatcherism and social care

The Thatcherite agenda on social care emerged in its community care policy, set out in the same 1990 Act as the NHS reforms (DoH 1990). Again, the discipline of the market was aimed at the agencies providing community care – mainly local authorities, but also the NHS and voluntary organizations. However, in the community care context the third strand of the Thatcherite approach to health and social care showed itself most clearly. It was here that individual clients found themselves placed by the state in the customer role – paying for their services, whether these are residential or domiciliary. And it was here that the private entrepreneur was most explicitly encouraged. Some encouragement was given to the private sector in the NHS, but in community care the government explicitly set out to foster the development of a thriving private sector, with the individual entrepreneur being seen as a particularly significant and welcome figure. However, even in this context the status of consumers was compromised by the fact that their payments were made to the local authority rather than to the provider of the care. The responsibility for individuals to make provision for their care was more clearly signalled in this sector than in any other. Thatcherite community care policy also gives some indication of the Thatcherite view of the relationship between the market and two other ways of mobilizing human resources – family obligation and voluntary activity. Despite the provisions of the public, private and voluntary sectors, it was generally acknowledged that the bulk of care is provided within the family. This kind of care is mainly provided by female relatives and draws on feelings of family solidarity and obligation. However, here Thatcherite policy was contradictory. As Pascall (1997) points out, family duty is in conflict with the effect of freer markets in the economy generally in pushing toward more demanding and insecure workplaces which were also part of the Thatcher agenda, and which on the whole put more pressure on women to work, allowing them less time for family activities. The same applies to voluntary activity in the community. On the one hand active citizens were praised. On the other, economic and workplace developments made voluntary activity more difficult (by lengthening working hours) and as Williams (1992) pointed out, the internal market in care forced voluntary organizations to ape commercial organizations and lose something of the mutuality, and indeed solidarity, that characterizes voluntary activity.

The Thatcherite project focused primarily on the deleterious effect of state intervention on individual responsibility. It never addressed the change that consumer culture brought about in relation to individual agency. As a government of the party of modern capitalism it was also a government of consumerism, and the commodification of personal, family and community life progressed apace in the Thatcher years (Walker 1989). The removal of state influence simply allowed more space for the influence of commerce to exert itself. Certainly the individual citizen was more fully converted to the consumer role in 2000 than was the case in 1979. The issue of health and lifestyle as addressed in *The Health of the Nation* (DoH 1992) is interesting in this context, as commercial interest in creating dependent consumers of tobacco, alcohol, unhealthy foods and polluting cars clearly conflicts with the health needs of those people. Agency depends on information, and the government never sought to balance the volume of misinformation presented to the population through advertising to encourage their continued unhealthy living. This seems to be a clear example of the conflict between the priorities of agency and the priorities of consumerism.

The New Labour response

New Labour has approached the issue of responsibility and solidarity in health and social care rather differently. Heffernan (1998) argues that it has accepted a good deal of the New Right analysis of state involvement in the economy and society in terms of its effects, and Powell and Hewitt (1998) suggest that there has been a more specific convergence with the Conservative view in relation to the welfare state. There has been real concern over the supposed corrosion of the willingness and ability of people to take responsibility (in terms of taking control, fulfilling duties and accepting accountability) for their lives and activities. New Labour also accepted that excessive state involvement in the economy had contributed to serious economic problems before 1979, and that Thatcherite policies had achieved some positive results in terms of making British producers more competitive.

However, New Labour did not share the Thatcherite view of the appropriate response to the problems that they agreed on. Thatcherite economic policy had helped British producers to become more competitive at a considerable price in terms of increased inequality and social deprivation, and New Labour has sought to address those problems while at the same time continuing to support and encourage enterprise and responsibility. It seems that New Labour is attempting to reconcile the two principles that concern this chapter – responsibility and solidarity. Their aim is clearly to encourage more responsible behaviour, but there is also a commitment to ensuring that the worst-off are not simply punished for their poverty but are supported to achieve full participation in the economy and society. The difficulties of reconciling these goals in practice explains the difficulty in agreeing policy in this area. Lister (1998) argues that there has been a shift of emphasis in New Labour policy from the principle of equality to the principle of inclusion, and it may be that this is the key to their attempt to reconcile responsibility and solidarity. Equality of outcome in terms of income and other rewards for effort must deny to some degree differences of input, and in that sense responsibility is compromised because the causal relationship between actions and outcomes in broken. However, inclusion – ensuring that nobody is excluded from the shared expectations of the community – could be seen as expressing the principle of solidarity without disconnecting people's actions from their outcomes, although it is not clear whether this will be the effect in practice.

Health care reforms have reflected this balance in a number of ways. The market principle has retreated significantly from the structure of the NHS and a duty of cooperation between commissioning and providing bodies has been put in its place. It is not as yet clear whether this will prove a more or less efficient way of providing health care. But it communicates an important message to health care workers and the population at large about the values that the government is seeking to express through the health care system. The rigorous and ruthless relationship of the market is being replaced by a relationship in which solidarity between different interest groups plays a significant part – though it may prove to be an imposed solidarity. Producer domination, which was ostensibly curbed by the internal market, is now to be kept under control by different mechanisms, in part consisting of duties laid upon the providers of health care to maintain professional standards. The government's health promotion agenda has shifted emphasis from individual responsibility and individual lifestyles to an agenda of inclusion. The White Paper *Saving Lives: Our Healthier Nation* (DoH 1999) explicitly seeks to strike a balance between individual responsibility for health and a communal responsibility for the management of those wider factors that affect health. This has involved a partial return to egalitarianism in relation to the reduction of class inequality in health status, which has become an explicit target. It is not clear how this relates to Lister's comment that New Labour is concerned with inclusion rather than equality. However, a commitment to remove health inequality amounts to a commitment to remove one of the ill-effects of socioeconomic inequality, which is not the same as a commitment to remove the underlying socioeconomic inequality itself. In fact, this might offer a model of social inclusion – to accept that luck and talent lead to different outcomes in terms of material wealth, but to acknowledge a collective duty to ensure that those differences do not exclude the less well off from a range of social goods. This position can also be seen as another balancing of solidarity and responsibility, recognizing a degree of individual responsibility for one's fortunes but recognizing also the need to express solidarity toward those less fortunate. Wainwright (1996) suggested even before New Labour came to power that the health inequalities debate was being revived at least in part because the egalitarian left was so weakened and discredited that discussion of inequalities in this context no longer challenged the basic acceptance of an unequal society. New Labour's approach to this problem seems to confirm that view.

State, family and community

I shall now consider the impact of the way the key principles of this discussion have been expressed in policy, on three key institutions – the state, the family and the community.

The state

The New Right's anxiety in the 1970s that the state was becoming more important in society has some basis in reality. There is no doubt that over a number of decades before 1979 the British state had shifted in terms of proximity from one model – the liberal state – to another, the statist model. As Schwarzmantel (1994) points out, for the liberal the state is a necessary evil, limiting citizens' freedom through policing, welfare and taxes, and it is imperative that its role does not extend too far beyond this. Rawls (1993) argues that it should be neutral in terms of moral values. The statist model by contrast involves a role for the state significantly beyond the limits of the liberal state, generally requiring intervention in economy and society, and corresponding use of a substantial part of the resources of society and economy. There are many reasons for this development. In the UK the beginnings of the statist model lay in the maintenance of a minimal level of public welfare, but the engine of state expansion in the early part of the twentieth century was war, and the need to mobilize resources for national survival. The social democratic version of statism (called by Cronin (1991) the 'liberal–socialist state') is only one version of this model, but it is distinctive in that it is propelled by a moral as well as a practical agenda. Unlike Rawls's model of the liberal state, the social democratic state is not morally neutral and exists to pursue actively the needs of its citizens; and it is committed to particular values that go considerably beyond the neutrality of the liberal state (Krieger 1999). These include equality and democracy, and generally also include values relating to the well-being of its citizens.

Most of the legislation that provides the main structures of health and social care in the UK has been the product of the mid-century social democratic agenda. In particular the main legislation creating the National Health Service and a national system of local authority-based social care was the work of the first Labour government in the UK with a clear majority and mandate. Subsequent Conservative governments accepted the systems created by this legislation. However, since the 1970s – particularly since the world financial crisis of 1973 which forced governments drastically to review their spending – the appropriateness of these policies has been increasingly questioned, first among conservatives, then among socialists. As modes of production have changed, the importance of the working class has diminished, together with its numbers. The poorest in society seem often not to have benefited greatly from government intervention in social and economic matters. Values of equality and solidarity seem to have lost some of their appeal to electorates. And governments have sought to reverse the trends of the previous decades, to limit the role of the state in social and economic affairs, to encourage individuals to take more responsibility for their lives; to accept greater inequality; to move at least some way back toward the liberal state. The Thatcher government (along with the Reagan administration in the US) pioneered this strategy, providing a model for other western states.

In opposition the Labour Party shifted somewhat from its commitment to the social democratic state model toward a position which is neither liberal nor social democratic. In some respects it is fair to say that New Labour's position is between these models, and tends toward one or the other on different issues. But there is some evidence of an attempt to move away from the polarity of the two positions. In terms of the relationship between citizen and state, New Labour seems to be seeking a model which strikes a balance between the state as agent of communal solidarity, and the state as enforcer of individual responsibility. Lund (1999) argues that New Labour is seeking to reconnect taxpayer and welfare recipient through a greater emphasis on social obligation. The concept of a contract between government, citizen and intermediate institutions seems an important one in New Labour's world-view (for instance in *Saving Lives*), and it is possible to see the influence of con-tractarianism here. In addition, the emphasis on citizen participation, and of a distribution of responsibility between state and citizen, carries with it an echo of the theory of the Civic Republican state (Galston 1993) – a model which has had little currency in the UK but which offers an alternative model to the liberal state, requiring as it does a limited state but also (unlike liberalism) an obligation of active participation by the citizen. Heron and Dwyer (1999) and Driver and Martell (1997) both see New Labour as taking on a communitarian position, strongly under-pinned by commitment to individual responsibility.

The family

The New Right analysts were correct in their view that the family was changing as an institution. Their view of causes and solutions are more open to dispute. Cheal (1999) records the shift in the first half of the twentieth century from family relationships based on a concept of duty to the 'companionate' family which by the middle of the twentieth century was well established. He suggests that this companionate family is a good deal weaker than the duty-based family of earlier times; that ties of affection are not as strong as ties of duty; and that the necessary structure of communal and social support that sustained family life may be diminishing at the same time. Beliefs about the family have shifted from a view of marriage and childrearing as being an almost inevitable part of living to a perspective that emphasizes the expressive aspect of family relationships – personal fulfilment, enjoyment and achievement. Giddens (1992) refers to the 'pure relationship' entered into by its par-ticipants simply for the personal rewards they expect from it (and term-inated when those rewards no longer accrue) as a developing model for such relationships. This seems to uncouple the relationship from the social supports and obligations which have traditionally characterized marriage. This also puts kinship ties in competition with other kinds of relationships based on choice and self-expression. It is perhaps no coincidence that that part of British society where kinship was particu-larly important – the traditional working class – has most dramatically retreated, both culturally and economically, over the past half-century. There seems no longer to be a consensus about the degree to which people ought to take responsibility for elderly or disabled relatives. Davies

(2000) reports that views supporting the accepting of such responsibility have retreated markedly over quite a short period of recent history.

The family occupies an ambiguous position in the responsiblity–solidarity axis. On the one hand the family is the basic unit of human solidarity. On the other, the idea of individual responsibility has traditionally included parental responsibility as a major component. The New Right saw the welfare state as undermining family responsibility, and the curbing of the welfare state was geared in part to force responsibility back onto families. However, as I suggested earlier, Thatcherite policies were contradictory, in that attempts to encourage family responsibility were matched by policies that, through their undermining of job security and working conditions, forced parents – particularly mothers – to give more time to work and less to their children. One might suppose that enforcing family responsibility was part of a larger enterprise of imposing a more rigorous, less self indulgent life in which the weight of individual responsibility in all sectors of life fell more squarely on the shoulders of the individual: a revival of instrumental agency. However, if this was the intention, it failed in this area at least. Individualism in its manifestation as a pursuit of individual fulfilment has not been excluded from the family arena, and attempts to enforce individual responsibility have been strenuously resisted, most notably in the case of the Child Support Agency where according to Millar (1996) the imposition of a more rigorous duty to maintain children of previous marriages clashed with the existing, somewhat contingent, view of parental responsibility among separated fathers.

The New Labour approach to the family has much in common with the Thatcherite approach in that the two-parent nuclear family is clearly seen as the most desirable model, and the New Labour aspiration is to frame policies to support this model. There is something of a tension in this area between the principle that parents have an irreducible duty to provide appropriately for their children if they are able – an idea that is certainly acceptable to some leading New Labour politicians including Blair himself – and the principle that the stability of the family is beneficial to all, and that the state should provide incentives for parents to do their duty, making it to some degree a matter of rational calculation.

The community

The ties of obligation that may have been characteristic of the traditional community have probably not been characteristic of many communities in Britain for at least a century. Despite this, some close-knit neighbourhood communities seem to have survived into the middle of the twentieth century, as evidenced by the work of writers such as Young and Willmott (1986) and Dennis (1969). However, the disintegration of such communities seemed to be visible even as they were being celebrated, as they were replaced by the suburbs inhabited by isolated nuclear families with little knowledge of their neighbours. The anxieties of writers such as Macintyre (1985) that liberalism denies the communal dimension of morality is echoed in a wider view that communities helped sustain a sense of shared morality and that their disintegration into a highly individualized consumer society threatens social cohesion and peace. Some writers of the New Right such as Dennis (1993) saw a need to remoralize communities alongside the remoralizing of families.

However, the concept of community goes beyond the idea of specific communities, whether neighbourhood or otherwise, to include also a kind of relationship and social bond which is not characterized by the intimacy of family, the impersonality of commerce or the formality of government. The concept of community can be extended to include a range of relationships and social bonds which exist between these other matrices and which have sometimes been characterized as 'civil society'. As Baker (1998) points out, civil society is a complex concept. However, it is generally understood to include relationships of varying formality from village cricket clubs to major national and international organizations. At the neighbourhood level such groups and organizations often provide the sinews of community involvement and communication. At a wider level they create a layer of activity free of both state and commercial contamination. The social developments of the last 25 years have to some degree presented a problem for the health of civil society as they have for the traditional neighbourhood in that suburban privatization tends to disincline people from engaging in voluntary activities in their spare time; and as Pahl (1995) points out, the changes in workplace norms in the past two decades simply leave less time for people to engage in community oriented activity alongside their other obligations.

Community and civil society played a very limited part in the strategy of the Thatcher and Major governments. It is clear that Conservative policies of these years contributed to the changing workplace norms that seem to have presented a problem for voluntary activity. Community care policy during these years encouraged the involvement of the private and voluntary sectors, and depended in practice on family care (usually provided by female relatives). But as Williams (1992) points out, voluntary organizations have had to change the basis of their operations somewhat to work effectively in the internal market for community care, and to become more like commercial organizations. This more 'businesslike' approach threatens to compromise the nature of the social bonds sustaining voluntary organizations.

The New Labour approach to the community suggests a substantial departure from Thatcherism. Promotion of the kind of voluntary, mutual relationships that sustain communities is high on the Blairite agenda and shows in a number of ways. It shows in health care in the community orientation of the health promotion policy in *Saving Lives* (DoH 1999) and also in the emphasis on the relationship between the community and the new key structures in the health service, the primary care trusts. Likewise the importance of civil society in New Labour's philosophy is considerable. The function of civil society in supporting the individual, the family and the community, in a set of relationships which emphasize agency and mutuality, in turn supports responsibility on the part of the individual and solidarity between individuals. New Labour's approach to the community reflects its approach to the state in that it is seeking to encourage a stronger sense of mutual obligation between citizens.

The future of health and social care

Looking to the future, a set of connected questions present themselves. The formal attempt to introduce market mechanisms into the health service has been reversed, but there is unlikely to be a return in the near future to the collectivist values of the mid-century in health and social care. Health care as a lifestyle issue – as an expression of expressive agency by the individual – is likely to continue to increase in importance as an area of individual choice and self-expression. However, health care as an issue of survival (physical or social) will not thereby lose importance, particularly with an ageing population whose choices may determine whether they remain in the community in old age, and may even determine their chances of survival through specific health crises. This is clearly the territory of instrumental agency. Questions remain as to which of this group of choices should be a matter of individual responsibility (with acceptance of individual consequences) and which should be a matter of collective responsibility; and whether collective responsibility should be the province of the state or of other collectivities such as the community. An interesting question also arises as to whether a consumerist culture focused on short-term symbolic gratifications can equip individuals to exercise responsibility in making instrumental choices about long-term viability and survival. Clearly the responsibility can be shared with others, and care can be organized in such a way that the burden of responsibility is always tempered by solidarity. However, anything short of a universal state system catering for all needs (which is a very unlikely prospect) will require some exercise of responsibility by the individual, in terms of initiating and negotiating provision. In order for this to be possible for most people, there needs to be a shared culture and set of relationships that sustains and legitimizes such transactions.

References

Baker, G. (1998) Civil society and democracy: the gap between theory and possibility, *Politics*, 18: 81–7.

Bunton, R. and Burrows, R. (1995) Consumption and health in the 'epidemiological' clinic of late modern medicine, in R. Bunton, S. Nettleton and R. Burrows (eds) *The Sociology of Health Promotion: Critical Analysis of Consumption, Lifestyle and Risk.* London: Routledge.

Capra, F. (1984) *The Turning Point: Science, Society and the Rising Culture.* London: Flamingo.

Cheal, D. (1999) The one and the many: modernity and postmodernity, in G. Allan (ed.) *The Sociology of the Family.* Oxford: Blackwell.

Cronin, J. E. (1991) *The Politics of State Expansion.* London: Routledge.

Davies, P. (2000) *Long Term Care.* London: Mintel.

Dennis, N. (1969) *Coal Is Our Life: An Analysis of a Yorkshire Mining Community,* 2nd edn. London: Tavistock.

Dennis, N. (1993) *Rising Crime and the Dismembered Family.* London: Institute of Economic Affairs.

DoH (Department of Health) (1987) *Promoting Better Health: The Government's Programme for Improving Primary Health Care.* London: HMSO.

DoH (Department of Health) (1990) *NHS and Community Care Act.* London: HMSO.

DoH (Department of Health) (1992) *The Health of the Nation: A Strategy for Health in England.* London: HMSO.

DoH (Department of Health) (1999) *Saving Lives: Our Healthier Nation.* London: HMSO.

Driver, S. and Martell, L. (1997) New Labour's communitarianisms, *Critical Social Policy*, 17: 27–46.

Edgell, S. and Duke, V. (1991) *A Measure of Thatcherism.* London: HarperCollins.

Galston, W. (1993) *Liberal Purposes: Goods, Virtues and Diversity in the Liberal State.* Cambridge: Cambridge University Press.

George, V. and Wilding, P. (1985) *Ideology and Social Welfare.* London: Routledge.

Giddens, A. (1991) *Modernity and Self-Identity.* Cambridge: Polity Press.

Giddens, A. (1992) *The Transformation of Intimacy: Sexuality, Love and Eroticism in Modern Societies.* Cambridge: Polity Press.

Gray, J. (1995) *Liberalism.* Buckingham: Open University Press.

Gray, J. (1997) *Endgames: Questions in Contemporary Political Thought.* Cambridge: Polity Press.

Habermas, H. J. (1996) Modernity: an unfinished project, in M. D'Entreves and S. Benhabib (eds) *Habermas and the Unfinished Project of Modernity.* Cambridge: Polity Press.

Heffernan, R. (1998) Labour's transformation: a staged process with no single point of origin, *Politics*, 18: 101–6.

Heron, E. and Dwyer, P. (1999) Doing the right thing, *Social Policy and Administration*, 33: 91–104.

Hutton, W. (2000) *New Life for Health: The Commission on the NHS.* London: Vintage.

Krieger, J. (1999) *British Politics in the Global Age.* Oxford: Polity Press.

Lee, M. (1993) *Consumer Culture Reborn.* London: Routledge.

Lister, R. (1998) From equality to social inclusion: New Labour and the welfare state, *Critical Social Policy*, 18: 215–25.

Lukes, S. (1973) *Individualism*. Oxford: Blackwell.

Lund, B. (1999) Ask not what your community can do for you: obligations, New Labour and welfare reform, *Critical Social Policy*, 19: 447–62.

Mabbott, J. D. (1966) *An Introduction to Ethics*. London: Hutchinson.

Macintyre, A. (1985) *After Virtue: A Study in Moral Theory*, 2nd edn. London: Duckworth.

Mill, J. S. (1962) Utilitarianism, in M. Warnock (ed.) *Utilitarianism*. London: Collins.

Millar, J. (1996) Poor mothers and absent fathers: support for lone parents in comparative perspective, in H. Jones and J. Millar (eds) *The Politics of the Family*. Aldershot: Avebury.

Pahl, R. (1995) Friendly society, *New Statesman and Society*, 10 March: 20–2.

Pascall, G. (1997) Women and the family in the British welfare state: the Thatcher/Major legacy, *Social Policy and Administration*, 31: 290–305.

Paton, H. J. (1978) *The Moral Law: Kant's Groundwork of the Metaphysic of Morals*. London: Hutchinson.

Powell, M. and Hewitt, M. (1998) The end of the welfare state? *Social Policy and Administration*, 32: 1–13.

Rawls, J. (1993) *Political Liberalism*. New York, NY: Columbia University Press.

Rorty, R. (1994) *Contingency, Irony and Solidarity*. Cambridge: Cambridge University Press.

Schwarzmantel, J. (1994) *The State in Contemporary Society*. London: Harvester Wheatsheaf.

Sennett, R. (1998) *The Corrosion of Character: The Personal Consequences of Work in the New Capitalism*. New York, NY: Norton.

Tawney, R. H. (1990) *Religion and the Rise of Capitalism*. London: Penguin.

Taylor, S. and Field, D. (1993) *Sociology of Health and Health Care*. Oxford: Blackwell.

Wainwright, D. (1996) The political transformation of the health inequalities debate, *Critical Social Policy*, 16: 67–82.

Walker, A. (1989) Community care, in M. McCarthy (ed.) *The New Politics of Welfare*. London: Macmillan.

Williams, A. (1992) *Caring for People: Caring for Profit*. London: London Voluntary Service Council.

Young, M. and Willmott, P. (1986) *Family and Kinship in East London*. Harmondsworth: Penguin.

chapter **four**

CONSUMERISM OR EMPOWERMENT?

In this chapter we explore two themes which are central to social policy and welfare. We draw out aspects of consumerism which are relevant in describing the position of users of services and consumer activity, engaged in by practitioners and welfare agencies, such as purchasing, contracting and responding to complaints. We then consider whether empowerment is a part of consumerism or whether it is a concept distanced from economic and commercial activities. This chapter also explores choice, paying for welfare and the rise of regulation. It ends with a brief discussion of cash versus care and explores the potential of direct payments for service users.

Consumers and consumption

The twentieth century saw a change in the language of social assistance from charity to welfare. The change can be portrayed as a move from people receiving support under the Poor Law, where they were assessed to see whether they were in need or truly destitute and unable to help themselves, to the ideas, following the Second World War, that a welfare state would help the less fortunate. Towards the end of the twentieth century the idea that people were entitled to support was more prominent and was seen as a recognition of their citizenship.

The languages of pauperism and consumerism are at different ends of the welfare spectrum. Paupers, receiving help from the Poor Law system, had little choice and the workhouse or parish relief systems systematically removed their privacy and dignity. Even in death a pauper's burial and grave were basic, feared and stigmatizing.

The reforms of the Second World War were designed to remove such elements of the Poor Law and to change the relationships between institutions and welfare agencies and their clients, patients or users. The introduction of the NHS, for example, symbolized this change:

> It will provide you with all medical, dental and nursing care. Everyone – rich or poor, man, woman or child – can use it or any part of it. There are no charges, except for a few special items. There are no insurance qualifications. But it is not a 'charity'. You are all paying for it, mainly as taxpayers, and it will relieve your money worries in time of illness.
>
> (Central Office of Information 1948)

Two elements distinguish this from pre-war health care and hospital provision: first, that the NHS was to be open to all and second, that, while 'free', it was not a charity but would be financed out of taxation.

With this bedrock the evolution of the NHS might have been one characterized by patient power. However, despite the potential for strong patient or consumer influence, it took many decades before patients exerted significant influence. There are a number of reasons for this:

- the dominance of professions such as medicine and nursing whose power, knowledge and status were not significantly reduced by the NHS: we can see examples of their power in case studies of hospitals where particular scandals or problems arose (see Martin 1984);
- the particular circumstances of patients whose illnesses may make them fearful, unconfident and reliant on professional goodwill and expertise;
- a lack of democratic control or influence over the NHS, which remained largely self-governing;
- professionals' accountability to their peers and the power of their own organizations and public image;
- a lack of systems for consultation and complaint with little but expensive legal redress for problems or mistakes;
- general public satisfaction and pride in the NHS.

Within other welfare sectors, consumer voices were similarly slow to emerge. The recipients of financial support might have become 'claimants' rather than paupers, but their position as consumers has not been so widely accepted. In contrast to most users of NHS services, those claiming social security benefits often are portrayed as:

- responsible for their own poverty;
- undeserving or scroungers;
- irresponsible and suspect (Alcock 1997).

Although Alcock noted that there are differences between those who are seen critically and those who are viewed sympathetically as the deserving poor (Alcock 1997: 9), it has taken some time for the language of rights and consumerism (in part) to exercise any influence on social security systems. The welfare rights movement and pressure group activities of the 1960s made some inroads into systems which were largely resistant to ideas of consumerism. Features of the social security system which contribute to its customers' lack of influence are different from the characteristics of the NHS and patient relationships. The social security system's claimants or customers have been seen as:

- lacking organization – with groups of single parents, unemployed people and disabled people particularly powerless until the 1980s and often reliant on charity for 'special help';
- stereotyped and stigmatized;
- lacking political and commercial influence;
- disadvantaged by features of age, gender and disability which may exclude people from positions of power;
- not surprisingly, lacking money or employment and the resources to command respect.

The NHS and social security systems differ in the extent to which professional expertise and authority and the trust placed in experts, such as doctors, influence the development of consumer voices. Both systems, however, have powerful systems of control and can draw their own boundaries around those who are deserving or entitled to their considerations.

It would be wrong to portray health service users and social security claimants as separate groups. People make use of a range of public and private services and so can have multiple identities as patients, claimants and customers. Being disadvantaged economically however, or poor, may increase the likelihood of becoming caught up in welfare or being seen as a social problem. This has been illustrated in studies of the relationships between poverty and ill health, such as the Black Report (Townsend et al. 1988). The experiences of individuals in respect of both areas of welfare are also reported in a range of studies. Marsden and Duff (1975), for example, found that unemployed men often reported problems with sleeping, eating and digestion, boredom and low morale. Later, Graham (1993) reported on the relationship between mothers and health-related behaviour such as smoking. She identified that women's economic and social hardships made cigarette smoking an attractive and affordable release of stress and element of pleasure.

Other studies have also noted that welfare services, particularly social security and social services, are largely 'consumed' by poorer sections of society. Schorr (1995) has identified one of the key characteristics of 'users' of local authority social services departments to be their low economic status. This is despite policy attempts to make social services a widely available or universal service. The report of the Seebohm Committee (1968) argued that the support of a social services authority would be beneficial for families with a variety of problems in whatever social circumstances.

While such policy was enacted in England and Wales by the Local Authority Social Services Act 1970, the optimism of the Seebohm Committee was never translated into reality. The harsh economic climate of the 1970s, with the oil crisis reducing growth in government expenditure, meant that social services were to remain a limited service and for poorer sections of society.

The power of the pound

In this section we discuss the extent to which consumers are characterized by having control over payment or finance and consider whether pure 'consumerism', where people buy services or items with money or its equivalent, is part of welfare. We look at social policies which develop ideas of payment, and those which have relied on services 'in kind', in which people receive a particular service such as a meal or food voucher, instead of money to spend on their own food.

In the first half or the twentieth century, British social policy in respect of financial support moved from provision of support 'in kind' such as the food and shelter (on a very basic level) provided in the workhouse or through outdoor relief to direct financial support, through pensions and national assistance. But from the Poor Law onwards, there was concern that the poor could not always be trusted with money and that they might not spend it wisely. The first recipients of old age pensions, for example, had to be of good character, and over the decades special help, particularly related to vulnerable people such as children, incorporated assistance not cash. For example, help in 'kind' for low income groups has included:

- milk tokens;
- free school meals;
- school uniform vouchers;
- free prescriptions (covering all pensioners and other low income groups);
- free dental/optical treatment.

Although there are extra costs in administration of these, the overwhelming aim of targeting help on the most vulnerable and needy (especially poor children) continues to outweigh, in government eyes, the possible stigma and administrative complexities.

Vouchers have their supporters and their critics. To some extent they represent a compromise between cash and care. They are also familiar in the commercial world, with vouchers for many types of social and leisure items (books, cinema, mobile telephones and so on). In respect of many welfare services, the idea of choice, so pertinent to the notion of consumerism, is highly restricted. In the same way that the term quasi-market (Le Grand and Bartlett 1993) was coined to describe the organizational reforms of the NHS and Community Care Act 1990, many welfare users are quasi-consumers.

The idea of a quasi-market was used to describe the limited choices available under the purchaser/provider split through the fundholding capacity of general practitioners. As the White Paper *Working for Patients* (DoH 1989) explained, GPs were to be able to consider a range of referral points, choosing between hospitals, for example, to meet the health needs of their patients. GPs could also, once awarded fundholding status by the local health authority, offer or commission a range of services such as counselling or minor treatments.

In such a system the position of patients as consumers was mainly limited to choosing their GP (not very practical in many areas). Glennerster (2000) has commented that the purchaser/provider split had to be considerably watered down because of professional and, to some extent, public opposition. The Conservative government, therefore, can be seen as promoting patient choice but meeting resistance to this idea of putting market forces explicitly into the NHS. In Conservative thinking at the time (summarized by Glennerster 2000), reform of the NHS could have been accomplished by:

- more private health insurance;
- an 'internal market' for healthcare;
- radical change to hospitals' status.

While the changes set in motion by the NHS and Community Care Act 1990 were radical, they affected internal relationships within the NHS more than the relationship of patients to the NHS. Glennerster (2000: 188–9) commented in respect of the limited scope of the reforms:

All this shows how far the public and the profession had absorbed the non-commercial ethic and philosophy of the founders of the service. Despite the service's failings any suggestion that it was to be 'privatised' touched a raw nerve. So, too, did the idea that some patients would get preferential treatment.

While the NHS reforms did not explicitly develop a patient identity as a consumer, another element of Conservative government policy identified elements of a consumer relationship. The development of charters as a means of clarifying the relationship between public services and their users was developed by Prime Minister John Major in 1991 to provide consumers with rights to information, complaint processes and redress.

Citizen's Charters now characterize many public services: health, long-term care and transport. In education, an early example was the Parent's Charter *You and Your Child's Education* (1991, revised 1994). Parents were officially informed of their rights to choose forms of education and their rights to complain. As David (1998) also noted, the charter also outlined parents' responsibilities:

> You have a duty to ensure that your child gets an education – and you can choose the school that you would like your child to go to [later changed to 'which school you would prefer your child to go to'].
>
> (1998: 295–6)

Lister (1998) has placed Citizen's Charters within a set of procedural or process reforms to welfare (p. 218). She has described them as 'representing principles of consumerism rather than citizenship' (p. 219) because such charters are limited to:

- setting out information;
- relying on individuals to complain;
- procedural rather than substantive decisions.

Lister has proposed that such rights need to be more enforceable and that users or consumers should be more involved in the process of decision making and service development:

> Thus, in incorporating a more dynamic and active conception of citizenship, which treats people as active agents rather than the passive recipients of rights, the principle of citizenship is promoted in terms of both outcomes and process.
>
> (1998: 219)

The 1990s can be seen as the decade of charters and their growth has been linked to ideas about the development of business-orientated public services as well as customer or consumer identities for service users. Gilliatt and his colleagues (2000) have observed how both left and right political parties have embraced this vision of moving patients, clients or users to a new status by a commitment to '[liberating] the user of public services from the role of passive recipient (or even victim) of producer-led services' (2000: 333–4).

Instead of Major's Citizen's Charter the New Labour government placed more emphasis on Best Value but still regarded consumer principles as a way of managing the relationship between public services and the public. For some, these moves may be cosmetic or an excuse for increases in paperwork. For users, improvements in attitude appear welcome. Others have joined Lister in seeing consumer charters as providing a smokescreen for real issues of power and democracy. Indeed, Gilliatt *et al.* have pointed to ways in which people have to take on further responsibilities as consumers, such as using alternatives to busy doctors, for example NHS Direct, or thinking carefully before making use of emergency services. Adopting a healthy lifestyle, making use of screening facilities, caring for ourselves where possible and watching for untoward symptoms are all examples of a devolution of responsibility to consumers. Gilliatt *et al.* developed the idea of a 'responsible consumer' who is knowledgeable of the service or product and plays a part in supporting the enterprise. Others have termed such ideas as do-it-yourself consumerism, whereby consumers take on skilled or expensive work. Gilliatt *et al.* suggested self-assessment of income tax liability as a good example of 'co-opting' consumers (2000: 347) into difficult tasks. They noted that the beneficiaries of such moves do not appear to be empowered consumers:

> As the balance continues to shift between what is normal for service managers to do, and what it is expected consumers should be able to do for themselves, the organisation achieves a greater deal of flexibility. Thus the organisation rather than the consumer is empowered.
>
> (Gilliatt *et al.* 2000: 347)

Consumers and users of social care

While the NHS may be portrayed as a quasi-market, the changes of the NHS and Community Care Act 1990 provided some elements of 'markets' with growing use of independent (voluntary sector and commercial, profit-making sectors) providers of social care. The government's White Paper *Caring for People: Community Care in the Next Decade and Beyond* (Secretaries of State 1989) explicitly welcomed the market of social care whereby choice for consumers was available through alternatives to public sector provision, notably private residential care homes and voluntary sector provision in day services. Part of the NHS and Community Care Act 1990 (section 52) also included great emphasis on people's rights to complain and extended this to include

- people directly or indirectly in receipt of services;
- people whose request for a service has been refused;
- people acting on behalf of the above.

A complaints system was to be set up that would be easily accessible, responsive, fair and impartial. In the event, the government was to locate much of this complaints system within the local authority, as well as, initially (although at arm's length) responsibility for registration and inspection systems for social care. Later on, government policy acknowledged the difficulties for local authorities in being inspectors of their own services or provision. In the Care Standards Act 2000 it established the National Commission for Care Standards to relieve local authorities of this difficult responsibility and in response to calls for independent inspection and regulation to enhance public confidence and trust.

The Conservative government was explicit about consumer principles. The Department of Health (DoH, SSI and Scottish Office 1991), in practitioners' guidance on care management and assessment, declared:

> The rationale for this reorganisation is the empowerment of users and carers. Instead of users and carers being subordinate to the wishes of service providers, the roles will be progressively adjusted. In this way, users and carers will be enabled to exercise the same power as consumers of other services. This redressing of the balance of power is the best guarantee of a continuing improvement in the quality of service.
>
> (1991: 9, para. 6)

Heavily influenced by production of welfare approaches which pointed to the advantages of targeting support on those most in need and most able to benefit from social care support, the Department of Health established a system of care management, where individual practitioners and social services authorities would undertake five key tasks:

- screening to see who is eligible for help or referral elsewhere;
- assessment of need, rather than suitability for existing services;
- planning an acceptable 'package of care' incorporating networks of support;
- reviewing the package to determine its suitability;
- monitoring the care received.

All such tasks were meant to be influenced by service users' wishes and choices, although the extent to which choice was uninfluenced by resources was so crucial that it formed the subject of court cases throughout the 1990s (see Chapter 9). While the government espoused principles of consumerism, it can be seen that, in reality, practitioners and social services authorities still held the major hand. Looking at the five tasks of care management listed above, for example, it is largely in the 'package of care' element that care managers had to make use of the independent sector. In the early years of implementation of the reforms, private residential care or independent domiciliary (personal and/or domestic support at home) schemes were 'purchased' by care managers but often as a result of a contract or agreement between the local authority social services department and the care provider organization. The notion of service users being seen as consumers, or treated as such, had its parallels with the NHS, with care managers operating as 'quasi-consumers'.

In essence, perhaps we should not be surprised that the consumer focus of the community care reforms was limited. They were a policy reaction to capping or controlling public expenditure on residential care for older people in particular which, until 1993 (the final implementation of the NHS and Community Care Act 1990), was financed for those with limited incomes and savings by the social security system. As Glennerster observed (2000), there was a paradox in the pre-1993 system which was 'an almost perfect voucher system that had grown up by accident' (p. 190) since it promoted choice and the flexibility of the market. A government committed to consumer choice had to find a new way to preserve some elements of this theme: it did so by insisting that the local authority care managers would have to purchase care or support, on behalf of service users, from the independent sector. In an early study of the implementation of the reforms, Ellis (1993: 9) noted:

> Consumer power is the centrifugal force which will inevitably focus the attention of providers on individual needs and preferences. But the analogy is weak. In terms of product development, purchasing power remains with the provider rather than the consumer.

In questioning the extent to which service users agree with some elements of consumerism, we can move beyond the labels to explore what people want from services and how these desires fit with ideals of consumerism. Two studies (Turner 2000 and Qureshi et al. 1998) have identified what is important to users of long-term support services and their carers. These include:

- choice about where to live and how to spend their days;
- having a say in treatment, care and support, and in the type and timing of services;
- access to employment and meaningful activity;
- support to participate in social activities and help in running the home;
- help to sustain family relationships;
- feeling safe and secure at home and in the neighbourhood.

As we can see, choice figures highly but so does support. It is also possible to identify themes arising from theories of normalization or ordinary living (choices, dignity, contribution, relationships and ordinary places). These five accomplishments (O'Brien and Tyne 1981) appear highly relevant to policy aims, although other policy imperatives, such as policies on equal opportunities, mean that they may need to be put into place with due regard to cultural or race issues. Consumer ideals can be interpreted very individually and this may not reflect wishes of communities where family needs are placed at high level.

As seen in the earlier section from the practitioners' guide on care management (page 58), there was often a tendency in the early days of community care to view the interests of users and carers as coinciding. Meanwhile, elements similar to consumerism can be increasingly seen in statements from service users or people with disabilities. These may not coincide with the views of their families, or the opinion of professionals. A statement of what people with learning disabilities want, for example, included the following:

- to make choices about where they live and who they live with;
- to have girlfriends or boyfriends of their choice and to have other friends;
- to make decisions about their own lives.

(Mental Health Foundation 1996: 5)

Such choices may be seen as impractical or unwise, or even harmful, by relatives or staff. The latter have to manage the dilemma of advocating choice but wishing to exercise control. This tension may explain why consumerism is less evident in mental health services than in other parts of community care. To be a consumer is associated with adult status and being able to make rational or sensible decisions. Some expectation of responsibility and consideration is evident. But for people whose insight is considered impaired in some way, and especially for those who are judged to be mentally ill and a risk to their own health or safety, or the health and safety of others, there are controls over their abilities to choose elements of their life. For example, the current Mental Health Act 1983 provides for people to be placed under the guardianship of the local authority or to be subject to supervised discharge after a period of detention in a mental health in-patient unit or hospital. They may be required to attend a certain venue for assessment or monitoring, and/or to live in a certain, specified place, and/or be required to admit a professional to monitor their well-being. New proposals, at the time of writing, to reform the Mental Health Act 1983 reduce people's ability to decline treatment or medication when living in the community.

Choice, then, as a central part of consumerism, is not absolute but very much depends on who is making the choice and how it will be paid for. Even though the social care 'market' has a range of providers, some restrictions of choice apply, for reasons such as:

- a lack of providers in certain areas, for example, in rural communities. One private social care provider may have a monopoly; for some areas local authorities have little or no provision of their own (in-house);
- financial ceilings on the amount of support a person is awarded so that, for instance, a person might be seen as 'costing too much' for support at home and encouraged into institutional care;

- conflict or disagreement about the type or level of support needed. A person might not wish to be helped to get ready for bed at 5 p.m. or might find that a 15-minute visit from a care worker to help with personal care is too rushed.

As a number of distressing accounts have revealed, choice in community care may be non-existent and the service provided may be abusive. The Longcare Inquiry (Buckinghamshire County Council 1998), for example, explored how residents of homes for people with learning disabilities were subject to the power of staff members and had few choices about their living conditions. Exercising choice presumes a safe and supportive circle of family and professional or paid support. It is easy to forget that rights to non-abusive or safe support services are essential before thinking about choices. Government policy in this area, such as the guidance on procedures and policies at local level contained in the guidance document *No Secrets* (DoH 2000), is one development acknowledging that people have rights to protection.

From consumerism to empowerment

The limitations of consumerism have been identified, and within social care, and to some extent health-related services, the language of empowerment became stronger in the 1990s. Adams (1996) has summed up elements of empowerment in a brief checklist as entailing:

- service user involvement from the outset in service development;
- users playing a key role in assessing their own situation;
- users having a say in how services are planned, managed and delivered;
- user control/consultation over the allocation of resources;
- user contribution to the evaluation of services.

Definitions of empowerment are many and varied but generally the term is used to mean that service users have more control or power over the services or support they receive. Barnes and Bowl (2001) have argued that it is appropriate to see empowerment as 'a process in which people develop "power to" take decisions, take actions, make choices, or work with others which they were previously unable to do'. Such a definition helps to get over problems about whether people can be given or granted power by professionals. It is particularly applicable to circumstances where people may be too ill or distressed to act as 'consumers'. One example of such empowerment is the limited but growing use of advance directives, where people can make plans about what they wish to happen to them in the event of illness or incapacity.

Empowerment and consumerism may at first glance seem to have much in common. Both describe a relationship with services or other material goods. Consumerism is more market focused, however, and in welfare the word is frequently accompanied by other terms; quasi or citizen, active or passive, willing or coerced, to reflect the complexities of the transactions involved. Adams (1996) places empowerment within a historical time frame, drawing attention to aspects of self-help, mutual aid and political struggle in the nineteenth century which link to empowerment. Over the twentieth century, other important values such as self-determination have influenced empowerment. Empowerment, therefore, may not be only in respect of services but part of a move away from state or official support.

The government's policy response to growing calls among disabled people, in particular, for independence and control over their own help or support has been to formalize and extent direct payments initiatives. These are systems providing cash not care for disabled people who use such money to purchase their own community care services. The Community Care (Direct Payments) Act 1996 has made it possible for local authorities to set up such schemes building on experiences of the Independent Living Fund and local authority pilot projects, incorporating third party arrangements. Early schemes were considered highly effective and popular by disabled people. Zarb and Naidash (1994), for example, found that disabled people viewed direct payments as:

- more reliable and effective;
- providing more choice and control;
- giving a wider range of assistance;
- more satisfying;
- providing higher quality support.

They calculated that such arrangements were, on average, 30 per cent less expensive than direct services.

Such schemes place disabled people in a consumer role, with its disadvantages and advantages. However, it is not all 'sink or swim', for local authorities still maintain some control and monitoring functions. Most seem to be supporting independent sector organizations to help administer schemes and provide assistance and advice to individuals thinking about taking on the responsibility (see, for example, Dawson 2000). New developments, suggested by Glendinning and colleagues (2000), may lie in the impact of direct payments on health care. Their study found that disabled people were already using their personal assistant to replace conventional, but often inadequate or inconvenient, NHS services. They observed:

> Users described how the enhanced control and independence derived from being able to purchase their personal assistance had improved their morale, psychological well-being and, in some instances, helped

reduce systems of mental ill-health. These benefits are important elements of the holistic concept of independent living. They also demonstrate how the quality and effectiveness of services necessarily include the *ways* in which services are delivered, as well as their content.

(Glendinning *et al.* 2000: 41, original emphasis)

Without mentioning the word empowerment, such accounts provide evidence that consumer-type relationships can be empowering to a degree. They also raise the question of whether the meaning of empowerment is shared between professionals and organizations.

Bernard (2000) has described how initiatives in self-help health care for older people can be considered at individual, organizational and community levels. Older people may be helped to relate health promotion messages to their own lives, but they can also raise health issues within services or communities. In this way empowerment can be linked to policies around health promotion and community development. Empowerment, like consumerism, does not necessarily have to be confined to individual relationships or transactions.

Other researchers (Barnes and Warren 1999) have pointed to new terms replacing consumerism and empowerment, including involvement, participation and partnership (Warren 1999. 119). Warren has observed that agreed and definitive meanings for such terms may be difficult for users and professionals to reach, pointing out that users often have different views of what is important or politically desirable. She has proposed that recognition of contradictions is important and that advocacy may be one way in which service users and carers can participate in services, but also over broader territories.

This chapter has outlined key concepts of consumerism and empowerment. It has explored aspects of each concept, noting that there are points of commonality as well as difference. New moves to provide cash instead of care are at early stages and we have much to learn about whether this consumer identity is experienced as empowering, and about group or collective experiences of empowerment.

References

Adams, R. (1996) *Social Work and Empowerment*. London: Macmillan.

Alcock, P. (1997) *Responding to Poverty: The Politics of Cash and Care*. Harlow: Longman.

Barnes, M. and Bowl, R. (2001) *Taking Over the Asylum: Empowerment and Mental Health*. London: Palgrave.

Barnes, M. and Warren, L. (eds) (1999) *Paths to Empowerment*. Bristol: The Policy Press.

Bernard, M. (2000) *Promoting Health in Old Age*. Buckingham: Open University Press.

Buckinghamshire County Council (1998) *Independent Longcare Inquiry*. Buckingham: Buckinghamshire County Council.

Central Office of Information (1948) *The New National Health Service*. London: HMSO.

David, M. (1998) 'Education', in P. Alcock, A. Erskine and M. May (eds) *The Student's Companion to Social Policy*, pp. 293–8. Oxford: Blackwell.

Dawson, C. (2000) *Independent Successes: Implementing Direct Payments*. York: York Publishing Services.

DoH (Department of Health) (1989) *Working for Patients*. London: HMSO.

DoH (Department of Health), SSI and Scottish Office (1991) *Care Management and Assessment: Practitioners' Guide*. London: HMSO.

DoH (Department of Health) (1991) *Care Management and Assessment Practitioners' Guide*. London: Department of Health.

DoH (Department of Health) (2000) *No Secrets: Guidance on Developing and Implementing Multi-agency Policies and Procedures to Protect Vulnerable Adults from Abuse*. London: Department of Health.

Ellis, K. (1993) *Squaring the Circle: User and Carer Participation in Needs Assessment*. York: Joseph Rowntree Foundation.

Gilliatt, S., Fenwick, J. and Alford, D. (2000) Public services and the consumer: empowerment or control?, *Social Policy and Administration*, 34(3): 333–49.

Glendinning, C., Halliwell, S., Jacobs, S., Rummery, K. and Tyrer, J. (2000) *Buying Independence: Using Direct Payments to Integrate Health and Social Services*. Bristol: The Policy Press.

Glennerster, H. (2000) *British Social Policy Since 1945*, 2nd edn. Oxford: Blackwell.

Graham, H. (1993) *When Life's a Drag: Women, Smoking and Disadvantage*. London: Department of Health.

Le Grand, J. and Bartlett, W. (eds) (1993) *Quasi-Markets and Social Policy*. London: Macmillan.

Lister, R. (1998) Principles of welfare, in P. Alcock, A. Erskine and M. May (eds) *The Student's Companion to Social Policy*, pp. 214–20. Oxford: Blackwell.

Marsden, D. and Duff, E. (1975) *Workless: Some Unemployed Men and their Families*. Harmondsworth: Penguin.

Martin, J. (1984) *Hospitals in Trouble*. Oxford: Blackwell.

Mental Health Foundation (1996) *Building Expectations*. London: Mental Health Foundation.

O'Brien, J. and Tyne, A. (1981) *The Principle of Normalisation: A Foundation for Effective Services*. London: Campaign for Mentally Handicapped People.

Qureshi, H., Patmore, C., Nicolas, E. and Bamford, C. (1998) *Overview of Outcomes of Social Care for Older People and Carers*, Outcomes in Community Care Practice Series, No. 5. York: University of York Social Policy Research Unit.

Schorr, A. (1995) *The Personal Social Services: An Outside View*. York: Joseph Rowntree Foundation.

Secretaries of State (1989) *Caring for People: Community Care in the Next Decade and Beyond*, Cm 849. London: HMSO.

Seebohm Committee (1968) *Report of the Committee on Local Authority and Allied Personal Social Services*, Cmnd 3703. London: HMSO.

Townsend, P., Whitehead, M. and Davidson, N. (1988) *Inequalities in Health: The Black Report and the Health Divide.* Harmondsworth: Penguin.

Turner, M. (2000) *'It is what you do and the way that you do it.' Report on user views on the introduction of codes of conduct and practice for social care workers by the four national care councils, commissioned from the Shaping Our Lives User Groups.* London: Office for Public Management.

Warren, L. (1999) Conclusion. Empowerment: the path to partnership?, in M. Barnes and L. Warren (eds) *Paths to Empowerment*, pp. 119–43. Bristol: The Policy Press.

Zarb, G. and Naidash, P. (1994) *Cashing In on Independence: Comparing the Costs and Benefits of Cash and Services.* London: Policy Studies Institute.

chapter **five**

CENTRAL PLANNING AND MARKET COMPETITION

Introduction

Planning and competition are not intrinsically opposed processes. It is perfectly possible, indeed advisable, to plan in a competitive situation, and planning can itself become a competitive process. But the two ideas have become models of opposing ways of dealing with certain problems, and we need to consider why this is. First, however, I propose to consider the two ideas in themselves.

Planning involves the modelling of the future in order to establish what actions will achieve given goals in that projected future. It also involves the mapping of a sequence of actions – connected, articulated and cumulative – which will act upon the projected future situation in order to achieve those goals. Any planning body, be it central government or a small voluntary or commercial organization, requires the best possible knowledge of its future environment in order to make rational predictions about cause and effect in that environment; and it needs a clear idea of its goals in order to focus the planning process. Planning theory in the public sector has drawn a good deal on the planning models developed by commercial companies to enable them to survive in competitive situations. It is clear from Bryson's discussion of planning in the public sector that the basic dynamics of planning in the two sectors have considerable similarity (Bryson 1988). The main difference lies in the mandate of the organizations involved. Companies in a competitive market situation have a mandate from their shareholders to maximize dividends, and all company activities, including planning, are geared to this end. The position of government is quite different. As

Klein (1998) suggests, governments do not have the luxury of a simple mandate or simple goals, and often they also lack a clear yardstick to decide what their appropriate goals are, and what constitutes achievement of those goals. Public corporations, local authorities and other public bodies such as health authorities have simpler remits than central government, but in practice they are often also subject to similar ambiguities concerning what constitutes a legitimate goal, and what constitutes evidence that a goal has been achieved. For a commercial company the final point of reference is the shareholder and the ultimate justification of any action is the maximizing of dividends to shareholders. For public bodies, as Bryson reminds us, the equivalent points of reference are those bodies and individuals who are generally termed 'stakeholders'. Their agendas are on the whole more varied and contradictory than are those of shareholders. All of this makes it difficult for public bodies from government downward to pursue clear and measurable goals. Without such goals, planning is a somewhat problematic process.

Although planning may be vital to organizations in a competitive situation, the very nature of competition means that the competitive encounter itself cannot be fully planned, and indeed planning at that level would destroy the point of competition. As Samuelson (1967) pointed out in his classic introduction to economics,

> a competitive system is an elaborate mechanism for unconscious co-ordination through a system of prices and markets, a communication device for pooling the knowledge and actions of millions of diverse individuals.
>
> (Samuelson 1967: 40)

The classic form of competition is that of the market, where producers seek to maximize their profits and dividends by achieving maximum market share with minimum costs of production. Competition must involve seeking to drive one's competitors out of business, and the spin-off from that is that all producers seek to produce the most, the best and the cheapest. In traditional economic theory this is the most effective means of maximizing productivity and overall wealth. It follows that the competitive environment must be to some degree unpredictable and unplannable in order to maximize the risks and rewards involved, and thus sustain the stimulus to optimum performance.

The relative advantages and disadvantages of the two methods of distributing goods and services are generally well rehearsed. Planning by state bodies in a democratic polity ostensibly reflects the priorities of the electorate in distributing such goods as state bodies control. The market will not necessarily reflect those priorities. On the other hand central planning is slow and cumbersome both in its determining of need and its response to changes in need. The classic market by contrast is quick to respond to demand and, if demand reflects need, then it can be said to be quick to respond to need. Any small shift in the willingness of consumers to buy a particular good will very quickly be reflected in levels of price and production. However, a problem lies in the connection between need and demand. The market relies on purchasing behaviour to indicate demand, and purchasing behaviour depends on the disposable resources of consumers. Where consumers have a need which cannot be met through their disposable resources, that need will not be reflected in purchasing behaviour and will remain an unknown quantity. This reveals one of the fundamental difficulties for planners, that of information. In order to plan effectively, planners must know enough about their environment – not just at present but in possible futures – to be able to predict the probable effect of particular actions. This kind of prediction requires abundant information, and getting that information has been the most important practical problem affecting state planners during the twentieth century. In Ham's view (1999) it was one of the major stumbling blocks to the introduction of rational planning in the NHS in 1974. Data concerning need, and data concerning the effects of previous interventions, are both notoriously difficult to obtain and interpret. This is a disadvantage of planning. But the converse disadvantage of the market is that information, though in principle simpler to get and interpret, is essentially misleading on the matter of need. Willingness to buy a given quantity of a commodity at a given price can to some degree be predicted, and can be very quickly and accurately recognized once it is being put into effect. But if the market is attempting to respond to need, as opposed to demand, it is none the wiser.

Planning has many levels, and Smith (1994) identifies four such levels, running from the level of strategic planning, concerned with the mission of the organization over the longest feasible timescale, to the level of action planning, concerned with month-by-month resourcing. Strategic planning connects closely with the processes of policy making in the welfare state, and to a significant degree can be understood through similar models. The main contrast in models of policy making – that between rational and incremental policy making – has been applied also to strategic planning by writers such as Abel-Smith (1994) and Ham and Hill (1993). The rational model of planning frames planning as a strategic process which connects aims and expectations in a coherent whole. Harrison *et al.* (1990) describe rational planning as an activity based on an integrated view of what is required and what can be achieved, pursued consistently over a significant period of time. Rational planning is essentially coherent and proactive. The incremental model of planning by contrast frames planners as reactive rather than proactive, responding to pressures and changing demands, and the planning process as one of accommodation and compromise. It is fairly clear from what has been said already concerning the public sector that we might expect incremental planning to be more characteristic of the public than the private sector, as the goals of public bodies are more diffuse than those of commercial companies, and the pressures of stakeholders will be more conflicting and inconsistent than the demands of shareholders in the private sector.

The tension between planning and competition as methods of organizing health and social care (and indeed of organizing many other social goods) is highlighted by the fact that they have generally been seen as competing ways of achieving largely the same outcomes. As Abel-Smith (1994) points out, health and social care are normally understood to be provisions where resources tend to fall short of need. So the issue centres around the best distribution of available resources to achieve maximum effectiveness for minimum cost. Abel-Smith also set the goal of equality alongside that of cost-effectiveness, arguing that meeting needs to the same degree across the population stands alongside meeting needs in the most cost-effective way possible. Equity and cost-effectiveness may not always be achievable through the same methods and measures, and the achievement of one may sometimes be at the expense of the other; but their status as fundamental and irreducible is readily arguable. For the purposes of this discussion another goal might also be considered at a different level – that of legitimacy. The best use of the resources available for health and social care must be one that is politically sustainable, in that it can only be achieved in the long run if it has legitimacy. Evidence from social psychology cited by Brockner and Siegel (1996) concerning public responses to distributive decisions suggests that the legitimacy of the method through which the distribution was made is of greater importance than the legitimacy of the actual distribution, and this seems to provide an additional yardstick of comparison between planning and competition.

Historical and political background

The opposition between planning and competition as means of organizing social goods has a long history. The two concepts can be seen as ideal types representing two ways of applying the fundamental principles of utilitarian social philosophy. The utilitarian principle – that the maximizing of happiness is the most legitimate and rational goal for human beings, as individuals and collectivities – provided powerful underpinning for the market principle in Britain. In its development by Bentham (1962) it rested on a view that all persons would seek to maximize their own happiness, and that on the whole the aggregate maximizing of happiness is most likely to result from people being allowed to pursue their individual happiness. Human beings were viewed by the founders of utilitarianism as the best judges of their own happiness and the best agents thereof. This philosophy provided a justification for the essential rationality of market behaviour, on the argument that the maximizing of happiness will be expressed in individual decisions about the use of personal resources which maximize income. This, taken together with the view that the multiplicity of individual decisions is the most efficient available engine of aggregate prosperity, constitutes the main argument for the position that the free market, allowing unrestricted buying and selling, is rational and right. However, as utilitarianism developed, its leading exponents such as Mill (1962) also understood that individual well-being cannot always be gained in a way that adds to everyone's prosperity. In Mill's view it is possible for some to be harmed by these processes, and it is possible also for that harm to outweigh the gains that result. To maximize happiness in certain respects it is necessary for the state to regulate individual activity through the law, and sometimes for the state to intervene in, or even organize, certain activities. Weiler (1982) argues that through the development of these ideas Mill influenced the direction of radical and liberal thinking to move from complete faith in the free market toward acceptance of the need for state intervention, to such a degree that the present utilitarian position, in Ryan's view, is that 'whatever the state can usefully do, it should' (Ryan 1991: 94). The earliest excursions of the state into public health in the 1840s were justified by an essentially utilitarian view that, while the free market is the best mechanism for maximizing well-being in most sectors, there are certain areas where the state is the most effective instrument, and it is therefore rational that the state should fulfil that role. So the view of state planning as a rational activity also has roots in nineteenth-century utilitarianism.

In the period between the 1890s and the 1970s the role of the state in the operation of industrial societies increased markedly, stimulated by political changes such as the growth in power of the industrial working class in the first half of the twentieth century. Cronin (1991) describes how the demands of total war and the impact of economic cycles (accompanied by the development of the tools of economic analysis to understand these) propelled government into a more proactive role. To some degree there was also a convergence between the behaviour of companies in the market place and of government. As the size of units in the 'free market' increased and the ideal of perfect competition disappeared in many sectors, government and business became accustomed to cooperating in the running of an economy that was at least partially planned. The essential utilitarian underpinning of this development remained, in the sense that in Britain the goal of maximizing the well-being of the population (linked to goals such as social stability) remained paramount. However, the economies of Britain and other western states have remained predominantly capitalist, and capitalism has continued to operate primarily on the market principle of competition. Most of the economy in the UK has remained in the hands of private companies, and those companies have competed for markets and sought to maximize their dividends to their shareholders. So the extension of state planning has been a partial one that has not transformed the ownership of the main assets of the economy.

In contemporary politics the virtues of planning and competition are underpinned by two very different political philosophies. Gray (1997) describes neo-liberalism, with its emphasis on individual autonomy, as providing the main arguments in support of unlimited market competition. In the neo-liberal view the market is the place where the risks and opportunities available to the autonomous individual are at their clearest and most calculable, partly because they can be quite legitimately translated into monetary terms. Liberty is in part the liberty to compete, and to take full responsibility for the consequences of one's competitive behaviour, whether that leads to prosperity or penury. In the strictest formulations of neo-liberalism, as for instance developed by Nozick (1974), the state is a necessary evil, existing to provide minimal but unavoidable protection to the market in the form of a legal system, public order and national defence. Interventions by the state in the market beyond these necessary functions are likely to disrupt and distort market mechanisms to the detriment of the overall level of well-being. Against the neo-liberal position Krieger (1999) identifies the social democratic tradition which places the state in the role of the primary agent of planning, pursuing the goal of a more rational distribution of goods and services than could be achieved by the market. The social democratic view is that market rationalism and utility are partial and superficial, and that market mechanisms create distributions of goods and services which bear no relation to the need for these goods and services, or to the ability to benefit from them. In the social democratic view a deeper kind of rationality can be achieved by the use of the state as a rational planner, ensuring that a particular range of goods and services are distributed in a truly rational manner.

The problem for social democracy is that there is not a clear and self-evident way of distinguishing between goods and services whose distribution should be decided by the market, and goods and services whose distribution should be centrally planned in accordance with explicit principles. On this issue social democrats throughout the industrialized world have occupied many different positions at different times. In recent decades the view that most or all social goods and services should be subject to central planning has retreated, and a view that planning should have a more limited role has gained ground. All the political parties in the UK have moved toward the diminution of planning in the last twenty years, though ranged in different positions on the continuum. The problem of distinguishing the goods and services suitable for planning from those suitable for market distribution remains, however. Areas at issue include health care, education, social care, social insurance, transport and housing, all of which have been at various times subject to distribution by state planning. The recent diminution of planning has not fallen evenly on all of these.

The presence of health care in this list is readily explicable. First, its importance to survival is fundamental, and the vicissitudes of life are most acutely expressed and represented in the threat of illness, and the inability to afford appropriate treatment. And second, health care is an expert good. As Hudson (1994) points out, most users of health care are not in a position to identify all their own needs or make sufficiently informed choices of health care provision to be in the position of fully rational consumers. The decision as to what is needed and what is appropriate has to be ceded to an expert. So health care, or at least that part of health care provided by experts such as the medical and nursing professions, cannot show, and has never shown, the full benefits of market forces. Another argument that has been used to select health care out of the market in recent years, offered by Daniels (1985), is that certain goods and services have to be distributed equally if competition for all the other goods and services in the economy is to be conducted fairly, on a 'level playing field'. Otherwise the moral underpinning of a competitive society is lost because some people compete with unfair disadvantages. Health care and education are clear candidates for special treatment in this way because deficits in either of these areas disable people in a competitive society. Fair equality of opportunity means equality of access to these fundamental goods. It should be noted that social care has never been distributed on market lines to any significant extent, but has been provided in two ways: informally as part of family and community support, or formally through the machinery of social control – particularly the Poor Law.

Planning and competition in health and social care

In recent decades the history of health and social care in the UK has been characterized by an intensification of the polarity between planning and market competition. Thirty years ago it would have been unlikely that a chapter with this theme would have been written, as the role of the market in this area would have been seen in the UK as relatively minor, and issues of debate would have centred round different planning agendas. However, things have changed dramatically with the resurgence of neo-liberalism within the Conservative Party, and the retreat of social democracy across the political spectrum. This change cannot be seen in isolation. The history of health and social care planning since the Second World War can be seen as a period of accumulating difficulty with the business of planning. The National Health Service as it was set up in 1948 had relatively primitive planning machinery and a poor information base, and for many years there is no evidence of serious attempts at rational planning. In Klein's account (1995) the planning that happened was incremental. Developments were piecemeal, often reactive, and heavily influenced by the power structure within the NHS which for the first two decades was dominated by hospitals, and by the medical profession. Attempts at large-scale planning were made, such as Powell's hospital plan of 1962, but these tended to highlight the difficulty of planning rather than its potential. By the 1960s it had become clear that this system was not adequate to the demands on the service. Health care was a constantly expanding part of national expenditure, but the piecemeal, unplanned nature of that expansion was largely reactive to the increasing demands placed on it. The 1974 reform of the NHS was intended to introduce rational planning and work toward an essentially utilitarian agenda of clear priorities, seeking to maximize the effectiveness of the service in improving health. A planning system was introduced into the NHS in 1976 which for the first time established a planning cycle in some ways comparable to those used by business. In 1977 one of the main disutilities of the incremental approach – the uneven and irrational distribution of health care resources across the country – was tackled for the first time with the setting up of the Resource Allocation Working Party, which worked for some years subsequently to equalize resources on a rational basis.

However, the planning environment changed rather quickly in the 1970s. The economic crisis arising from the oil embargo in 1974 led to increasing pressure for limitations on public expenditure, and the expansionary situation of the 1950s and 1960s was replaced by a situation of stringency. In Klein's view the political conflict arising from this undermined the consensus necessary for rational planning, and Small (1990) argues that in this situation rational planning was not possible. Instead planners engaged in 'decremental planning' – a set of manoeuvres partly to ameliorate and partly to conceal the effects of financial stringency. In addition Ham (1999) points out that the planning system introduced in 1976 quickly ran up against problems of planning at authority level (often partly resulting from lack of available information) and of resistance from powerful interest groups, particularly sections of the medical profession. As a result the planners had to shift from a directive to a guiding system. Overall this looked rather like a reversion from rational planning to incremental planning. However, on the positive side of the equation these difficulties led to a greater emphasis on an activity which can be seen as central to rational planning – that of prioritizing. The financial problems of the 1970s made prioritizing imperative. At this stage the information base for making prioritizing decisions remained poor, however, as much activity under the direct control of the medical profession had never been subjected to systematic evaluation.

Although the resource crisis created problems for strategic planning, it was accompanied by the development of more rational planning at other levels – particularly business planning and budgeting. In the 1970s the public sector moved toward the adoption of a more managerial approach to the running of public services – active management as opposed to the administration that had characterized earlier decades. The proactive manager was seen as an appropriate person to run the machinery of the NHS in a period of stringency, and management as a methodology was strengthened in the NHS during the 1980s by the introduction of the general manager following the Griffiths Report (Griffiths 1988). However, this development did not resolve the problem of long-term strategic planning in the NHS, and developments on the political front ensured that it would be overlaid by wider changes. The problems for public finance created by the economic problems of the 1970s were affecting most western countries, and major public provision such as health care was coming to be seen as a real threat to the ability of advanced economies to regain economic viability. The increase in expenditure on health care had been an ongoing process, fuelled by demographic change, rising public expectations, and the developments and demands of medicine and the medical profession. Increasingly these were coming to be seen as inefficient, and Barker (1996) points out that this concern was developing throughout the western world. These developments were seen as a problem across the political spectrum, but the problems associated with state intervention in society and economy also provided the stimulus to an upsurge of neo-liberalism in right-wing parties throughout the west, and a return to market-oriented thinking. This represented a loss of faith in the prospect of rational planning by the state and public bodies and a growing suspicion that such bodies were vested interests, whose expansion at the expense of private enterprise would continue as long as was permitted. The non-productive nature of public bodies was contrasted with the wealth-creating role of the private sector, justifying a significant change of emphasis in favour of the private sector – a change which, as Francome and Marks (1996) point out, impacted strongly on health care.

The internal market

The most important result of this development for health and social care – the introduction of the internal market – was not primarily concerned, at least ostensibly, to return health care to the private sector, but was meant to import certain features of the market into the public sector. Glennerster (1998) calls the internal market a 'quasi-market' and argues that it was essentially a compromise, with an impact significantly more muted than that of full-scale privatization. However, the internal market was not simply the lowest common denominator of conflicting agendas. It was a concept with its own logic, and had in Enthoven (1985) its own theorist, whose ideas influenced policy makers at a crucial time.

The logic of the internal market rests on the introduction of certain of the processes of the market into an existing administrative structure, in order that transactions within that structure which were previously characterized by other dynamics are now characterized by the dynamics of the market. It requires that units compete for business rather than have work allocated to them on administrative lines. It requires also that they make a profit, or at least break even, rather than be expected to spend an annual budget allocation. The purpose of an internal market is to use the advantages of the market mechanism to optimize the operation of a public service. Those advantages were argued to be as follows:

- Service providers are induced to provide the best possible value through competition.
- To do this, they must be efficient.
- To do this, they must also be flexible, responding quickly to the requirements of the market as these change.

The idea that it is possible to achieve an optimum mixture of market elements and non-market elements within the same system of delivery is not new in health care. The mix of elements in the US system of health care has changed and evolved over the years, and the system of managed care, through which privately provided options were selected and regulated by non-profit-making organizations, is one model of this, as discussed by Robinson and Steiner (1998). However, in the US system the market is the starting point, and restriction and regulation have been introduced with the aim of containing the worst drawbacks of the market while retaining the stimulus of competition. That is the aspiration. In practice the US system is notoriously expensive and planners and politicians struggle to contain costs. In the UK the starting point in 1990 was a public system, and the plan was not to privatize this system, but to introduce the disciplines of competition into that public system. The system was divided between purchasers and providers. The purchasers, mainly health authorities, local authorities and fundholding GPs, had an explicit public mandate to ensure the availabililty of health care and community social care. The providers – NHS trusts, local authorities, voluntary and private bodies – were the organizations whose behaviour was intended to be most market-like, in that they would compete for contracts from the purchasers. That competition would maximize efficiency.

However, the discipline of the market is based on certain conditions that are not easy to reproduce in an internal market. First, units must be able to compete effectively. In rationally planned organizations units will be deployed with as little overlap of function and territory as possible, because this is efficient in that context. But in a market there must be overlap in order to enable competition. Two units must be able to serve the same population of customers in order to compete for their business. Ideally, considerably more than two units need have the potential to access the same customers. And the discipline of the market must involve real threats and opportunities. Ultimately a company that fails to keep its customers will also fail to remain solvent, and will go out of business. The prospect of unemployment is a powerful incentive on the part of executives and employees to work efficiently. An organization with an internal market must be willing to impose an equivalent discipline on the traders therein. This might not involve dissolution, but must involve a comparable incentive to produce and trade efficiently. Conversely, units that produce and trade efficiently must have the prospect of real rewards.

None of these conditions were met in the UK internal market after 1990. Because trusts were not allowed to borrow or go bankrupt under the 1990 system, the discipline of the market did not apply to them in an effective way. As Light (1999) points out, losers were not allowed to lose, and this meant that winners were also not allowed to win. Ease of entry into the market, in Light's view, was another crucial market characteristic which was absent from the NHS internal market. In fact there was not really enough overlap between different trusts for them to have to compete. Too many trusts had a virtual monopoly in their locality. If it had been easier for competitors to expand their operations in order to challenge someone else's territory, this would have introduced real competition. If it had been easier for new providers to break into the market this also would have enabled genuine competition. But neither of these elements was present, and therefore competition was compromised.

There are other ways also in which the NHS was unable to create the advantages of the market. Raftery and Stevens (1994) point out that the flow of information necessary to optimize the benefits of the market is unlikely to be available in the NHS. Their economist's ideal of 'perfect information' is in fact unlikely to be achieved in many settings, but the NHS is exceptionally remote from that situation. Certainly, as Light (1999) suggests, purchasers were generally working with woefully inadequate information at least in the early years of the internal market. This also limits competition. For competition to maximize efficiency it requires customers who can accurately assess the degree to which they are getting value for money in every transaction, and make purchasing choices on that basis. The lack of information available to health authorities meant that they were not in a position to make these assessments and were not therefore able to act as rational customers finding the most efficient provider. Even the providers themselves had difficulty in realistically pricing their products, as Glynn (1995) points out, because they did not have enough information about their own internal costs, thus compromising the market principle yet further.

Inevitably, under these circumstances, the impact of the introduction of the internal market was muted. The initial experience of becoming an NHS trust, and of working within defined financial restraints, seems to have been responded to positively by many trusts. Despite lack of competition, the pressure to control costs was real. However, the other side of the coin – the incentive to maximize quality – was by contrast much weaker. The key to this discrepancy seems to lie in the problem of information, as mentioned above. One response to the information problem was to focus on the measurement of process factors rather than outcome factors – speed of treatment being perhaps the major factor in this respect.

The internal market also created something of an ambiguity in terms of accountability. Denizens of the true market are usually accountable initially to their shareholders. State providers are accountable to the state. Some providers in the internal market experienced a highly ambiguous situation in this respect. A major feature of the internal market in health care was the attempt to devolve responsibility from central government to the trust level. The principle of 'subsidiarity' was, as Gray and Jenkins (1995) point out, a vital part of the Conservative government's strategy to devolve substantial parts of the existing state apparatus to agencies which, while remaining finally accountable to government, enjoyed substantial day-to-day independence. NHS trusts bore a relationship to central government which allowed central government (specifically the Department of Health) to divest itself of day-to-day responsibility for health care provision. The media and opposition parties resisted this shift of accountability with varying success and sought to hold central government accountable when things went wrong. It is not clear how far accountability was genuinely relocated in the eyes of the public. But the NHS trusts themselves experienced intense exposure in some cases. Given the nature of media exposure and media priorities, this was not always conducive to a quality product.

Glennerster (1998) argues that the period of the NHS internal market did see some real improvements in the performance of the NHS but that the contribution of the internal market to these is not always clear. He identifies some limited evidence that GP fundholders were a relative success in achieving better patient care and also greater efficiency and communication with trusts. He suggests, however, that the introduction of district-based purchasing did little to achieve more locally responsive health care. A reduction in waiting lists between 1989 and 1997 could be explained more easily by an increase in funding than by the operation of the internal market. Mays *et al.* (2000), in a similar analysis, present a very similar picture, with some gains for fundholding GPs and their patients, but otherwise little measurable change that can be clearly attributed to the internal market. However, they add that there was a major qualitative change in culture and relationships in the NHS, though this is not measurable quantitatively.

Beyond the internal market

The internal market is no longer the guiding principle of health and community care, but the Labour government elected in 1997 has not returned to the centralized planning of the 1970s. They have retained important parts of the market structure, while eschewing market relationships within that structure, and prescribing an entirely different set of relationships. Light (1999) argues that the great step forward achieved by the 1990 reforms was not competition, which failed, but the dividing of commissioner from provider, which still offers the promise of success. He envisages a managed, cooperative relationship between commissioners and providers somewhat on the lines of Japanese capitalism. The latter analogy is perhaps not as alluring now as it might have been a decade ago. But the idea may still have something to offer. The pre-1990 NHS was a system for producing health care. It was dominated by the values of production, and the consumer (the patient) was, by contrast, powerless to influence what was provided, and how. The 1990 reforms shifted the dominance of the producer by creating purchasers, quasi-customers who existed to meet the needs of the real consumer. The balance between production and consumption changed. This change also changed the balance of power in a different way. In the old NHS the power arising from control of the purse strings and the power arising from control of the machinery of delivery were inextricably, and indistinguishably, intertwined. In the 1990 system the two sources of power were separated and located in different places, with the purchasers/commissioners controlling the money and the providers controlling the machinery. So in two ways power was decentralized. The Labour government has reasserted a degree of centralizing direction, but the dispersal of power has not been anything like fully reversed, and many of the actions of commissioning and providing bodies are still guided by broad principles rather than day-to-day direction.

The main question is whether the principle of the market must be replaced by a principle equally, or more, effective in achieving the rational provision of health care. Hunter (1997) argues that the pre-1990 system was characterized by trust, shared values, openness and long-term commitment – qualities he believed were replaced in the internal market by a calculating watchfulness and dissimulation. One way forward might be to seek to restore the kind of relationships that existed before 1990 in Hunter's view. However, this may not be possible. The relatively cohesive society that produced the NHS in 1948 is gone for ever and Klein describes a corresponding loss of cohesion, and retreat from shared values in the NHS in the 1970s. Baldock (1999) argues that as a result of wider social and cultural changes there is now no consensus in society on the purpose of the welfare state. It seems that the 1990 reforms simply accelerated a process which was already well under way.

Looking to the future

This chapter started by identifying utilitarianism as the philosophical basis on which rational decisions about health and social care are possible through either the market or central planning. Utilitarian rationality depends on the possibility of a shared understanding of what is desirable and justifiable in terms of maximizing human well-being. It may be that the social and cultural changes of recent decades make such a shared understanding an unrealistic goal. Though in some ways humankind is more homogeneous through globalization, individual and group life priorities are generally becoming more diverse. Their definitions of, and recipes for, well-being are less and less likely to be reducible to a set of national priorities. In addition, the principle of rationality has to be reconsidered in the context of the complexity of information which organizations have to deal with. Ham (1999) argues that 'bounded rationality' is the reality in much of health care, with rational decision making bounded by restrictions in information, in the ability to process information, and in the ability to interpret information in its context. It may be that the utilitarian foundation for health and social care priorities, which justified both central planning and the market, is obsolete.

Baldock (1999) argues that the present government, finding itself presiding over a fragmented postmodern culture with no shared aspirations concerning welfare, has abandoned the project of a coherent welfare system in favour of inconsistent piecemeal reforms. If it is true that there is no longer a basis for common priorities, a different strategy is needed, and it may be that despite Baldock's pessimism, a different strategy is possible in health and social care. It is noticeable that the government has given considerable attention to redefining the relationships required between organizations in health and social care, and that concern with these relationships may offer a way forward. If shared goals are no longer viable, it may be that the shared values of health and social care can nonetheless focus on the means whereby goals are arrived at, and the relationships that underpin that process, rather than the goals themselves. A culture which sets principles in place for the *way* organizations deal with one another to arrive at goals for their output may be an alternative to the culture of consensual goals. One such principle might be that of cooperation, given statutory force by the latest legislation. Another might be that of organizational responsibility for standards of professional practice, embodied in the principles of clinical governance. It remains to be seen whether principles such as these and the machinery that go with them can provide a template for the kind of interorganizational relationships which would allow rational health care provision, in a way that improves on the flawed rationalities of centralized planning and the market. The problem of arriving rationally at shared moral goals in late modern society is a fundamental issue affecting all public arenas and many private ones, and possibly the most coherent treatment it has received is from Habermas (1991), who sought to replace Kantian rules of individual moral reasoning with a system of communicative ethics allowing protagonists to arrive at shared moral goals in a rational way. These were intended for individuals, but there is an equally pressing need for a framework for organizations to engage in the same quality of dialogue, and Habermas's system may provide the basis for this.

However, the framework of interorganizational relationships must include not only the norms of communication, but the bonds of obligation within which that communication will take place. If a culture of obligation and dialogue is an adequate replacement for the utilitarian culture of collective goals, and given the nature of late modern organizations, this culture could only be sustained by an overarching regulatory regime provided by government. It is not clear as yet how far or how deeply the government sees into this issue, and how coherent their response to this need will be in the long run. Only time will tell.

References

Abel-Smith, B. (1994) *An Introduction to Health: Policy, Planning and Financing.* London. Longman.
Baldock, J. (1999) Culture: the missing variable in understanding social policy, *Social Policy and Administration*, 33: 458–73.
Barker, C. (1996) *The Health Care Policy Process.* London: Sage.

Bentham, J. (1962) Introduction to the principles of morals and legislation, in M. Warnock (ed.) *Utilitarianism*. London: Collins.

Brockner, J. and Siegel, P. (1996) Understanding the interaction between procedural and distributive justice, in R. Kramer and T. Tyler (eds) *Trust in Organisations*. London: Sage.

Bryson, J. M. (1988) *Strategic Planning for Public and Non-Profitmaking Organizations*. San Francisco, CA: Jossey-Bass.

Cronin, J. E. (1991) *The Politics of State Expansion*. London: Routledge.

Daniels, N. (1985) *Just Health Care*. New York, NY: Cambridge University Press.

Enthoven, A. (1985) *Reflections on the Management of the NHS: An American Looks at Incentives to Efficiency in Health Services Management in the UK*. London: Nuffield Provincial Hospitals Trust.

Francome, C. and Marks, D. (1996) *Improving the Health of the Nation*. London: Middlesex University Press.

Glennerster, H. (1998) Competition and quality in health care: the UK experience, *International Journal for Quality in Health Care*, 10: 403–10.

Glynn, J. (1995) Financial management reform in the NHS, in J. Glynn and D. Perkins (eds) *Managing Health Care: Challenges for the 90s*. London: Saunders.

Gray, A. and Jenkins, B. (1995) Public management and the National Health Service, in J. Glynn and D. Perkins (eds) *Managing Health Care: Challenges for the 90s*. London: Saunders.

Gray, J. (1997) *Endgames*. Cambridge: Polity Press.

Griffiths, R. (1988) *Community Care. An Agenda for Action*. London: HMSO

Habermas, J. (1991) *Communication and the Evolution of Society*. Cambridge: Polity Press.

Ham, C. (1999) *Health Policy in Britain: The Politics and Organisation of the National Health Service*. Basingstoke: Macmillan.

Ham, C. and Hill, M. (1993) *The Policy Process in the Modern Captialist State*. London: Harvester Wheatsheaf.

Harrison, S., Hunter, D. and Pollitt, C. (1990) *The Dynamics of British Health Policy*. London: Unwin Hyman.

Hudson, B. (1994) *Making Sense of Markets in Health and Social Care*. Sunderland: Business Education Publishers.

Hunter, D. (1997) *Desperately Seeking Solutions*. London: Addison-Wesley-Longman.

Klein, R. (1995) *The New Politics of the National Health Service*, 3rd edn. London: Longman.

Klein, R. (1998) Can policy drive quality?, *Quality in Health Care* 7 (Supplement): 51–3.

Krieger, J. (1999) *British Politics in the Global Age*. Oxford: Polity Press.

Light, D. (1999) Policy lessons in the British health care system, in F. Powell and A. Wessen (eds) *Health Care Systems in Transition: An International Perspective*. London: Sage.

Mays, N., Mulligan, J. and Goodwin, N. (2000) The British quasi-market in health care: a balance-sheet of the evidence, *Journal of Health Service Research and Policy*, 5: 49–58.

Mill, J. S. (1962) Utilitarianism, in M. Warnock (ed.) *Utilitarianism*. London: Collins.

Nozick, R. (1974) *Anarchy, State and Utopia*. New York, NY: Basic Books.

Raftery, J. and Stevens, A. (1994) Information for purchasing, in J. Keen (ed.) *Information Management in Health Services*. Buckingham: Open University Press.

Robinson, R. and Steiner, A. (1998) *Managed Health Care*. Buckingham: Open University Press.

Ryan, A. (1991) Merit goods and benefits in kind. Paternalism and liberalism in action, in T. Wilson and D. Wilson (eds) *The State and Social Welfare*. London: Longman.

Samuelson, P. (1967) *Economics: An Introductory Analysis*. New York, NY: McGraw Hill.

Small, N. (1990) *Politics and Planning in the NHS*. Buckingham: Open University Press.

Smith, R. (1994) *Strategic Management and Planning in the Public Sector*. London: Longman.

Weiler, P. (1982) *The New Liberalism: Liberal Social Theory in Great Britain 1889–1915*. London: Garland.

chapter six

CONTROLLING SERVICE DELIVERY: PROFESSIONALISM VERSUS MANAGERIALISM?

Introduction

This chapter examines the sociopolitical context of 'welfare professionalism' in the UK, focusing upon the 1980s and 1990s. It considers tensions in its relationship with the role of the state and towards the concept of managerialism, particularizing factors such as professional identity and the context of professional decision making. Much contemporary discussion of welfare professionalism has been set against a 'culture of denigration' (*Guardian*, 12 April 2001) within public services generally, whereas the broader context is the backlash against professional society at three levels:

- against the power, privileges and pretensions of special interest groups, especially the organized professions;
- against the unstoppable growth of 'big government' with the attempt to 'roll back the state' by cutting public expenditure and privatizing nationalized industries;
- against corporatism, the involvement of special interest groups, above all employers and trade unions, in the framing of government policy.

(Gladstone 2000: 16)

Managerialism as a contrasting element is evaluated both as a progressive social force and as ideology rooted in scientific management and public choice theory. Recently its ideas have been connected with culture management, entrepreneurship and public sector governance, away from hierarchy and bureaucracy towards contract. The political attack on welfare professions begun during the 1980s has been accompanied by more regulation including increased control over activities of clinicians and efforts to reorganize the workforce of both health and social care sectors. The Labour government elected in 1997 has introduced an NHS Plan to achieve higher levels of professional recruitment, retention and more customer accountability. Professionalism in the context of partnership has been chosen as a political antidote to resolving long-standing efforts to integrate service provision and make it more user-responsive.

Professionalism

The organizational construction of the British welfare state was structured by a commitment to two modes of coordination: bureaucratic administration and professionalism (Clarke and Newman 1997: 4). Through this settlement notions of public service – as a set of values, a code of behaviours and forms of practice – became institutionalized. Professionalism provides a sharp contrast with bureaucratic administration which emphasizes predictability, stability and regulation. The idea of professionalism instead stresses the 'indeterminacy' of social interactions as necessitating the intervention of expert judgement. Problems demand expert knowledge and lay perspectives lack such expertise. There have, however, been recent counter-claims which stress the salience of the evidence-based practice movement as an alternative to authority-based practice, characteristic of much professional work (Dawes 1994; Gambrill 1999, 2000). This process involves increased client access to information and involving clients as informed participants along with considering their values and expectations.

Where bureaucracy operates through the standardization of work processes clearly delineating roles and responsibilities, professionalism is based on the standardization of skills through externally controlled training and qualification (Mintzberg 1983). Professionalism lays claim to an irreducible autonomy – the space within which professional judgement can be exercised, trusted and by inference is accountable:

> Professionalism operates both as an occupational strategy, defining entry and negotiating the power and rewards due to expertise, and as an organisational strategy, shaping the patterns of power, place and relationships around which organisations are coordinated.
>
> (Clarke and Newman 1997: 7)

Expanded welfare provision has meant closer and meaningful dialogue with professional groups. It is generally assumed that professionals have become indispensable partners in national social reconstruction given that social problems and social needs are recognized as complex entities not responsive to simple political and administrative solutions.

An exception is where managerial solutions have through political fiat been given precedence in spite of professionals' wishes. Professionalism has in the past been actively sought by politicians defining the boundaries of the welfare state as it concerns applying expertise for the public good (the notion of the professional placing his or her skills or expertise at the state's disposal in pursuit of a common interest). This represents the consensual, 1940s–1970s view of the welfare state sustained by an agreed neutrality: a bipartisan political settlement which proclaimed the welfare state as above party political differences; a bureaucratic administration which promised social impartiality; and support for professionalism which promised the application of valued knowledge in the service of the public.

Macdonald's (1995) sociological analysis of professions focuses upon the role of the state and includes a structural approach to professionalism: how groups of people professionalize and how professionalism can be defined, drawing upon earlier work of Johnson (1972, 1982) which concentrated upon a typology of professions. Some sociological accounts of professionalism yet seem to dismiss the term as rhetoric. To achieve status and monopolistic position in the market for services of some kind, aspiring professionals need to stress the distinctness of their knowledge, the undoubted authenticity of their altruism and the responsibility of their members (Deverall and Sharma 2000: 25). Macdonald (1995: 133) singles out factors affecting the position and practice of caring professions: mediation, knowledge, indeterminacy and patriarchy. Caring professions are mediative because they operate in conditions where a third party mediates in the relation between producer and consumer, defining both the needs and the manner in which the needs are met (Johnson 1972: 46).

The crux with respect to power relations is that welfare professions' activities are defined by the state – both the needs they are to deal with and the way in which those needs are to be met; and furthermore, their funds are provided by the state (Macdonald 1995: 134). This limits their power and their dealings with other occupational groups and weakens their position in negotiating economic rewards. Where the product of their activities is not clearly defined, their position is weakened still further. For instance the government-sponsored analysis of community care delivery led by Sir Roy Griffiths (1988) argued in favour of care being relatively mechanistic and undemanding of high levels of professional skill; his conclusions proved hence unsupportive to the professionalization argument.

The problem of defining outcomes of caring professions hinges on their so-called knowledge base (true professions are said to possess esoteric knowledge). There is a considerable body of opinion that holds that practice is actually the more important aspect (see Mackay 1990: 34). This emphasis on knowledge derives from 'trait' theory, which relied heavily on the delineation of the characteristics which were held to constitute a profession. This formed the dominant perspective in early studies of professionalism (Greenwood 1957; Carr-Saunders and Wilson 1962; Etzioni 1969; Toren 1972) and one which reflected the views of established professions. Each occupation to be considered as a candidate for the label 'professional' could be compared to the list of traits, and the degree to which it matched was then taken as an indication of the extent to which that occupation was professionalized. In an essay originally published in 1915 entitled 'Is social work a profession?' Flexner ([1915] 2001) reviews six criteria: professions involve essentially intellectual operations with large individual responsibility; they derive their raw material from science and learning; this material they work up to a practical and definite end; they possess an educationally communicable technique; they tend to self-organization; they are becoming increasingly altruistic in motivation.

One of the principal reasons why the trait theorists identified nursing, social work and the remedial professions as 'semi-professions' is that they do not appear to have developed dominance in discrete areas of knowledge (Hugman 1991: 104). Yet professional attributes are claimed as the symptom and not the cause of an occupation's standing (Howe 1986: 96). According to this view, professionalism is limited by the success in gaining power over such factors as an area of knowledge and associated autonomy, rather than limited by the intrinsic nature of those factors. The greater the element of judgement required in the exercise of professional knowledge, namely 'indeterminacy', the less likely it is that the professional tasks will be open to routinization and inspection. To take examples of nursing and social work, both require considerable exercise of judgement in their practice. However, the exercise of judgement in these cases is on the basis of knowledge that both the lay public and adjacent professions may not see as being sufficiently esoteric to take it into the true realm of 'indeterminacy'; being 'everyday' rather than professional knowledge (Macdonald 1995: 135). This view can appear narrow and outdated as it fails to take account of the growing body of theoretical work now claiming to underpin professional practice.

The idea of patriarchy has been significant in influencing the identity of caring professions (Larkin 1983; Witz 1992): the values of patriarchal society are built into institutions, and its practices shape and reinforce the belief among its members that they have a vested interest in maintaining such values. Aspects of nursing and social work tasks are already socially defined as appropriate for women. Those taking up these roles accept that their position within the organization will be strengthened and secured by adhering to their predefined role. Early developments of occupational associations, for example nursing, were based upon a 'probationership' model as a means of acquiring occupational knowledge;

consequently the emphasis (in nursing) is on dedicated caring and concern as opposed to academic training.

Health care professions have been 'tormented by two incompatible views of professionalism' (Fish and Coles 2000) in the late 1990s. On the one hand they have been urged to undertake reflective practice (something which many claim they have 'always done'). On the other hand, the concerns of bureaucrats for continuous quality improvement (CQI) and total quality management (TQM) have imposed on their work system-wide procedures such as protocols and guidelines. These require professionals to follow rules and discourage independent thinking. Fish and Coles (2000: 285) refer to these as the professional–artistry view and the technical–rational view of professionalism respectively.

The technical–rational view emphasizes labelling everything in mechanistic terms, conceptualizing professional practice as a basic matter of delivering a service to clients through a predetermined set of clear-cut routines and behaviours. The term 'delivery' is taken from the commercial sector; it presents professional practice as a non-intervening 'agent for conveying safely something created by one body to another' (Fish and Coles 2000: 291). As the market model and its variants have become more dominant, professional work has become more controlled by the dictates of performance measurement. Restraining public services is believed to empower the consumer. The technical–rational approach to health care of prescribing all the practitioner's activities is said to cut down considerably the risks incurred when professionals make more of their own decisions:

> Here the ever-present threat from accountability has been allowed to push the practitioner into such a defensive frame of mind that he or she is constantly in a 'no-win position', where both to act and not to act are equally likely to invite litigation, and where it is only possible to defend activities which come within the pre-specified rules. And it assumes that practice is a relatively simple interaction in which the practitioner gives and patients and clients receive, and which can be perfected.
>
> (Fish and Coles 2000: 292)

The professional–artistry view of professionalism contrastingly believes that the technical–rational concept denies the real character of both professionalism and practice:

> Far from being simple and predictable, professional practice involves a more complex and less certain 'real world' in which, daily, the professional is involved in making many complex decisions, relying on a mixture of professional judgement, intuition and common sense, and that these activities are not able to be set down in absolute

routines, or be made visible in simple terms, and certainly not able to be measured, and which because of this are extremely difficult to teach and to research.

(Fish and Coles 2000: 293)

However we define professionalism, descriptions of the welfare state have assumed that a combination of bureaucracy and professionalism 'supported a particular ideological representation of the relationship between the state and the people in which (professionals) served as the institutional guarantors of the pursuit of the public good' (Clarke and Newman 1997: 118). This perception has changed somewhat radically.

Managerialism

During the 1980s in the UK managerialism was presented as the means through which rigorous discipline could be introduced to the public sector to produce cost-effective public services. This identification of management as being business-like, as the driving force for greater productivity, efficiency or 'value for money', is based on a fairly general conception of management as a progressive social force (Clarke and Newman 1997: 34).

The broad recasting of public sector management, according to Clarke and Newman (1993: 428), is so significant as to constitute a transformation, occurring as part of an 'agenda of managerialisation which aims to make management the driving force of a competitively successful society'. As part of the new contractualist agenda in public administration, the state sector has been subjected to increasingly intense forms of managerialism, captured largely in the theoretical framework of the new public management (see, for example, Aucoin 1990; Hood 1991; Hood and Jackson 1992; Gregory 1995; Boston et al. 1996). This involves closer alignment of public sector governance with its private sector counterpart, by seeking to introduce more market imperatives into the operation of the public sector, including making changes to the sector's structure, its ownership and regulation and its management techniques. It also demands shifts in the mode of provision of public services away from hierarchy and bureaucracy towards contract, so as to 'let the managers of public service agencies manage'.

The new public management contains several important elements: a greater focus on (most often quantifiable) results or outcomes as opposed to (qualitative) processes; an elevation in the concept of 'management' at the expense of the traditional construct of 'administration', thus reinforcing the objectives of waste minimization and efficiency enhancement in the use of public resources; the devolution of management control and increased accountability on the part of public servants; the separation of commercial from non-commercial public sector functions and the detachment of policy advice from delivery and regulatory mechanisms; a significant stepping-up of contestability in, and contracting out of, traditionally publicly provided services, with an increased use of tightly specified and often shorter-term, outcome-focused contracts; and a boost in the emphasis on monetary incentive schemes and cost-cutting measures (Boston *et al.* 1996: 26; Rhodes 1997, 1998; Ramia and Carney 2001).

The managerialist public sector is rooted in specific theoretical perspectives, particularly public choice theory, which offers a framework using (economic) rationality in decision making as the main criterion (North 1990; Levi 1998). In addition managerialism is given credence by the so-called 'new institutional economics' which highlights the minimization of transaction costs as the major policy and strategic imperative (Bryson and Smith-Ring 1990; Kettl 1993; Boston *et al.* 1996) and by agency theory, or the theory of principal and agent, which focuses on the law and policy considerations surrounding the nexus between a principal, the party who instigates contractual relations and the agent, who performs a function for the principal in return for a reward (Althaus 1977; Perrow 1979). The last of these, agency theory, enshrines a regulatory framework marking out the disaggregation of the public sector, mainly through a complex of legal and quasi-legal agreements between public sector organizations and between public and private ones. This forces sections of the public service to interrelate contractually with private and other public sector organizations, a restructure known in the UK as a 'quasi-market' (Le Grand and Bartlett 1993; Bartlett *et al.* 1998).

The 1980s and 1990s witnessed an ideology of managerialism as promoting the way forward for western economies experiencing economic decline and stagnation in the face of global change and competition. It presented 'culture management' as the right response necessary for changing the face of an organization which 'announced the possibility of a way forward which linked the fortunes of the individual manager, the corporation and the nation' (Clarke and Newman 1997: 35). This new managerialism built upon ideas of F. W. Taylor (1911) and Charles Perrow (1979). It propounded a vision of scientific management applicable to all kinds of human activities, best known for time and motion techniques and for studies of detailed movements of workers dealing with particular, well-defined tasks. Scientific management constituted

> a clearly-marked complex that ties together patterns of technological innovation with techniques of organisation and larger designs for social change, unifying its entire structure with an ideology of science as a form of puritanism.
>
> (Merkle 1980: 11)

The general approach of scientific management (e.g. Henri Fayol) is summarized by Self (1972: 21):

a) the central problem is one of co-ordinating an elaborate system in which full opportunity ought to be taken of the advantages of specialisation

b) to assist effective specialisation, principles must be discovered for breaking down and allocating the tasks of government among different departments or agencies

c) to ensure effective performance, responsibilities must be defined and clarified and 'unity of command' must be secured. This implies that the whole system will follow a clear hierarchical pattern, whereby subordinates will take orders from only one superior and the 'span of control' will be rationally settled

d) to assist planning and co-ordination, 'staff services' have to be inserted at appropriate points in the hierarchy, particularly at the top of the structure. These staff services have to be properly defined and located, and reconciled with the principle of unity of command.

The 'scientific management' theorists can be criticized on two points (Self 1972: 27). First, there is an unwarranted emphasis on the values of a disciplined hierarchy. Fuller understanding of social behaviour suggests that organizations can generally function at least as effectively, and can provide better personal satisfactions to their members, when structured more flexibly. Other factors besides formal structure hold an organization together and enable it to work harmoniously, e.g. strong personal relations among managers. Second, theorists neglected diversity of organizational context which led them to expect too much of organizational 'principles'.

Herbert Simon (1945) sought an alternative approach to administrative efficiency through designing a rational model of decision making. He employed a framework of applied behavioural research, quantitative measurement and social science method to understanding organizational dilemmas. His argument ran that in any situation an administrator ought ideally to examine all possible courses of action open to him or her, trace through the consequences of each alternative course, and then separately evaluate the benefits and losses of each alternative. He or she should then choose that course of action which is expected to provide the greatest net satisfaction. Simon contended that this model is superior to the traditional ends–means approach by which most administrative action supposedly proceeds. A full description would require all the relevant ends to be specified, either as aims to be pursued or as constraints to be observed. This requires the construction of a 'goals matrix' whereby the relative importance and mutual compatibility of these various goals is first determined. Simon's contention that the decision itself is too gross a unit for analysis, and must be broken down into decision premises, opens up examination of all the physiological, psychological and sociological factors, including training and acculturation, which shape the behaviour of individuals taking decisions (Self 1972: 48).

Decisions, systems ideas and organizational introspection, like scientific management, extensively penetrated government and the public sector but influenced some parts of this sector more than others (Pollitt 1993: 305). Their presence was most noticeable in the training of general administrators and in the general administrative, planning and policy formulation units of state, local and city government. The language of systems – 'feedback', 'inputs', 'environment', 'interface' etc. – was widely learned and used, even where the impact of these concepts went little beyond rhetoric (Pollitt 1993: 307). Criticisms of the decisions and systems perspective rested on its incapacity to address the inherent complexity of social action and the realization that differing perceptions of organizational 'realities' prevailed. The need was to recognize the primacy of individual ethical choice over the normative imperatives entailed in institutions (Reed 1988: 37).

'Culture management' became fashionable in the 1980s:

> Just as the human relations school had reacted against the mechanistic model of the individual deployed by the Taylorists, so the culture management advocates (Peters and Waterman: In Search of Excellence, 1982, Charles Handy: Understanding Organisations, 1976) believed that most decision-theoretic and systems analyses neglected the importance of symbolism and ritual in organisational life.
>
> (Pollitt 1993: 308)

This was not just a process of organizational restructuring but a large-scale process of cultural change through which 'hearts and minds' could be engaged. The emphasis of culture management moved to designing changes which aimed to produce new incentives rather than simply being enforced (Clarke and Newman 1997: 36). Change then becomes a task to be 'self-managed' rather than a series of centrally driven restructurings: the focus moved to creating the conditions which require everyone to become a 'change agent'. Organizational activities hence become suggestive of visionary images of change, i.e. customer driven, empowering staff, delivering quality services and so forth. For organizational professionals, old conceptions of progress where the professional 'solved' social problems have been displaced by a more limited vision of 'more effective service delivery', 'improved customer responsiveness' or 'enhanced performance'.

The spirit of managerialism and entrepreneurship hence becomes a metaphor for reinvention involving a fundamental transformation in ways of thinking how an organization might respond to a situation or given problem. Greater autonomy involved the possibility of becoming more responsive and flexible, for example hospitals converting to trust status (following the National Health Service and Community Care Act 1990) were able to apply their resources creatively and more independently. Managerialism has reshaped the role of (bureau-) professionalism, according to Clarke and Newman (1997: 76) through means of displacement, subordination and co-option. Displacement and subordination for example might take the form of influencing professional judgement by the requirement that the process takes account of the realities and responsibilities of budgetary management. Co-option more robustly involves management disciplining professional autonomy by subjugating professional discourse, for example in the area of 'quality', and pursuing its own understanding of the term through corporate missions and strategies. The maintenance of standards and dissemination of good practice were more naturally professional concerns in the past but have become the principal diet of managers in the language of performance indicators, comparative league tables, audit and evaluation.

The political attack on welfare professions

When the New Right came to power in 1979 it was set on ending the traditional world of welfare professionalism. Foster and Wilding (2000) analysed how, for instance, doctors, social workers and teachers have been subjected to increased political as well as managerial controls over their areas of work. The New Right constituency saw the professions as a powerful vested interest, effectively accountable to no one – politicians, managers or consumers. They were inefficient as a result of their insulation from market forces competition and ineffective in resolving health and social problems, e.g. poverty/social exclusion. This criticism has been specifically directed at social workers and local government officials including criticism of their expertise and ethic of service which was seen as tenuous and amorphous by attacking politicians and New Right supporters. Concerns over health care professionalism, such as maintenance of standards, costs and variations in practice, have been voiced in the literature (Kassirer 1993; Newble *et al.* 1994; Southon and Braithwaite 2000). Allegations about health professionals' performance include a slow uptake of new knowledge and practice, a high error rate (Leape 1994), interprofessional rivalries, a preoccupation with professional rights and remuneration, a lack of willingness to be accountable and, generally, a neglect of patient interests.

To take the case of health provision: the first significant move to rein in professional power was the introduction of general management to the NHS following the Griffiths Report (Griffiths 1983). This report

> took a mere six months to complete its task. It worked quickly and informally, consulting a great many people but not taking any formal evidence. It thus marked a break with the tradition of setting up Committees and Royal Commissions, representative of all the interested parties, whose job it was to produce acceptable consensus reports: a break which was one of the hallmarks of the Thatcher administration. The new management style in the NHS was thus born of an equally new approach to decision-making in Government – brisk and decisive, if sometimes also peremptory – and mirrored many of those characteristics.
>
> (Klein 2001: 124)

The diagnosis of Griffiths was that the NHS was suffering from 'institutional stagnation'; health authorities were being 'swamped with directives without being given direction'; the NHS was an organization in which it was 'extremely difficult to achieve change'; consensus decision making led to 'long delays in the management process'. The introduction of general management meant extending political control as well as asserting managerial power. It began a direct challenge to medical hegemony and signalled a sustained attack on other health professions, insisting that they be more accountable.

The Griffiths prescription entailed a general management structure from the top to the bottom of the NHS – i.e. individuals, at all levels, responsible for making things happen. At the top, within the Department of Health and Social Security (DHSS), there was to be a Supervisory Board to be chaired by the Secretary of State, to set objectives, take strategic decisions and receive reports on performance. Below that, but still within the Department, there was to be a Chief Executive, to carry out the policy objectives, provide leadership and control performance. Lastly, there were to be general managers responsible for the operations of the NHS at all levels – regions, districts and units. The general managers, the report suggested, might well be recruited from outside the NHS or the civil service, while their pay should be linked to their performance.

The post-Griffiths era was thus marked by a more assertive management style towards the NHS workforce. Nurses, for instance, quite clearly lost out: the effect of the Griffiths recommendations was that nurses lost both the right to be managed exclusively by a member of their own profession and their automatic representation on district management teams, both guaranteed by the 1974 corporatist arrangements (Klein 2001: 127). The medical profession was attacked over its self-governing status, involving a major review between 1988 and 1990 and the introduction of a new contract for general practitioners.

Working for Patients (DoH 1989b) extended management control over clinicians in its coverage of consultants' contracts including, for instance, detailing the number of outpatient clinics a consultant was expected to hold and the allocation of merit awards. *Working for Patients* created an internal market where groups of professionals were forced to compete with each other for business partly dependent on the expertise of managers to develop the bids and cost contracts. This approach demanded collaboration from doctors. The intellectual basis of this 1989 White Paper

> which appears to owe a good deal to the ideas of Enthoven (1985), is the assumption that a system of internal markets, in which NHS health care institutions compete with each other, will produce both greater efficiency and greater responsiveness to users. The creation of such an internal market entails the separation of two functions which are at present conflated in the role of district health authorities: the provision of hospital and community health services, entailing the ownership of health care institutions and the employment of direct care staff, and the purchase (or commissioning) of care, that is, the allocation of funds to providing institutions so as to ensure that the needs of a population are met.
>
> (Harrison *et al.* 1990: 169)

It was a new kind of relationship and the implications of the purchaser–provider split served to justify a new level of managerial activity in what had previously been no-go areas for managers (Harrison and Pollitt 1994: 122). The renegotiation of what was meant by clinical autonomy or freedom – and how the demarcation line between managerial and professional responsibilities should be defined – was to continue into the 1990s and is still far from completed (Klein 2001: 130). A further threat to hospital consultants stemmed from the rising interest, commencing in the 1980s, in techniques designed to measure the relative impact of different procedures in terms of the cost of achieving specific outcomes. So, for example, one study compared the quality-adjusted life years (QALYs) yielded by heart transplants as against by-pass surgery (Buxton *et al.* 1985). The collectivist utilitarian origins of the NHS became functionally embodied in the views of economists and epidemiologists and such an analysis ran counter to the ethical individualism of the medical profession.

In 1990 new contracts were drawn up and finally imposed on GPs, reconstituting Family Practitioner Committees as Family Health Service Authorities to whom, for the first time in their history, they became managerially accountable (Calnan and Williams 1995: 222; Foster and Wilding 2000). General practitioners became required to work within indicative prescribing budgets, to meet targets for vaccinations and immunizations and cervical cytology. The subsequent 1997 NHS Primary Care Act provided health authorities with new powers to circumscribe boundaries of primary care and actively develop policy in this managed area. The political opposition to professional autonomy was advanced during the 1990s by 'the transformation of NHS patients into consumers' (Klein 2001: 178). For the NHS, there was *The Patient's Charter* (DoH 1991a) which set out a series of rights, ranging from the right 'to receive health care on the basis of clinical needs, regardless of ability to pay' to the right 'to be guaranteed admission for treatment by a specific date no later than two years from the day when your consultant places you on a waiting list'. The Department of Health followed up *The Patient's Charter* in 1994 by publishing a comparative performance guide showing the extent to which individual hospitals (and departments within them) had achieved its standards as well as various performance targets set by the NHS Management Executives, for example increasing the proportion of people treated as day patients. 'Hence consumer politics were replacing producer politics' (Klein 2001: 190).

The centre playing a more active role in shaping performance at the periphery became a central theme of the newly elected Labour government's White Paper, *The New NHS: Modern, Dependable* (DoH 1997). The White Paper introduced the notion of 'clinical governance' – measures directed at strengthening systems of professional self-regulation to run parallel to managerial systems of quality control (Glendinning 1998: 158). National service frameworks would be produced, drawing on the best available evidence, to provide a mission and focus for the organization of services. A National Institute for Clinical Excellence was to be set up to promote, bring together and diffuse evidence about good practice – 'a sign of the government's view of the need for outside pressure to maintain standards of professional work' (Foster and Wilding 2000). The Labour government's notion of modernization and permanent revisionism, promoting entrepreneurship and innovation, represents a sustained questioning of professionals' performance and particularly focuses upon professional demarcations in public services. Some of the main reforms are articulated in the NHS Plan (DoH 2000a) and in *A Quality Strategy for Social Care* (DoH 2000b), both of which identify workforce issues as central to bringing about change and improvement.

New Labour's initiatives to 'modernise': examples NHS Plan and *A Quality Strategy for Social Care*

In a lecture delivered at Green College, Oxford over the growing tension between professionalism and accountability in public services, Labour

MP Tony Wright, Chair of the Public Administration Select Committee, asserted that in future:

> We require a dual relationship, professionalism respecting account-ability and accountability respecting professionalism. We need to expand and revise our definitions of what professionalism is, i.e. one that is prepared to measure itself against a public interest test: a willingness to share expert knowledge; a commitment to work with others on common issues; a willingness to engage with lay people on equal terms; to accept scrutiny and transparency and to find the capacity to respond to the new world of disappearance of deference.
>
> (Green College Public Health Lecture Series, 29 January 2001)

These statements appear to encapsulate New Labour's approach to welfare professionalism by continuing the Conservatives' reforms towards achieving greater accountability within public services. They omit drawing a distinction between 'full professions' (for example, doctors, lawyers) and 'semi-professions' (for example, social workers, teachers, nurses, police), where in the case of the latter issues of recruitment, retention, inadequate pay coupled with low levels of training and education are currently endemic. The NHS Plan focuses upon investment in staff – 7500 more medical consultants, 2000 more GPs, 20,000 extra nurses and 6500 extra therapists; and is aimed to redress 'a lack of national standards, old-fashioned demarcations between staff and barriers between services, a lack of clear incentives and levers to improve performance and overcentralisation and disempowered patients' (Summary, NHS Plan). Extracts from the NHS Plan (DoH 2000a):

> The biggest constraint the NHS faces today is no longer shortage of financial resources. It is shortage of human resources – the doctors, nurses, therapists and other health professionals who keep the NHS going day-in and day-out.
>
> (Para. 5.2)

> It takes years to train doctors, nurses, therapists and other health professionals. Our ability to expand the NHS workforce is still being constrained by the limited investment made by the previous government in education and training for the future of the NHS.
>
> (Para. 5.3)

> These are very challenging targets but we must meet them – and if possible exceed them – if the NHS is to make the service gains for patients they need. We will achieve them by:
>
> - increasing throughput from training
> - modernising pay structures and increasing earnings

- improving the working lives of staff
- recruiting more staff from abroad.

(Para. 5.5)

Inadequate resources and resultant lowering of morale have continued to be the complaints made by NHS professionals who criticize disruptive managerial change, introduction of inappropriate commercial techniques and politicians 'losing the plot' on the direction of the NHS. It was subsequently reported (*Guardian*, 19 December 2000) that 'disappointing pay increases' promised for 2001 would not be enough to attract staff needed to implement the NHS Plan (following the Health Secretary, Alan Milburn's announcement that he accepted the pay review body's recommendation of a 3.7 per cent rise for nurses and therapists and 3.9 per cent for doctors and dentists). This is likely to become a major tension for implementing the NHS Plan as recruitment, retention and career development are essential requirements. Extending consideration of how to make public services more effective was elevated as a main policy aspiration throughout the general election campaign of 2001. A backlash to years of formidable managerialism has resulted in serious workforce depletion in most areas of public services.

In the view of the professional associations, improved pay, better working conditions and incentives are needed urgently. If the government is to succeed with the NHS, it needs to find a means for recruiting and retaining professional staff in the long term rather than 'quick fix' solutions:

The new NHS Plan aims to 'design services around the patient' and make major changes in the way that professionals in the NHS work. This means that rather than a relatively small number of large-scale and generally managerial changes, the plan relies on making a very large number of relatively small changes in the detail of how the NHS and its professionals work.

(*NHS Confederation Viewpoint: NHS Plan*, Issue No. 1, August 2000)

An example of such small changes is proposed in the area of nursing pay: giving midwives with a year's satisfactory service access to progression from the top three pay points of Grade E to the top of Grade F without the need for promotion; topping up the pay of staff in areas where there are labour market shortages by introducing a Market Forces Supplement, for example in London; and by furthering pay incentives 'for those prepared to work flexibly' (DoH 2000a: para. 5.14). Managers are to be rewarded for 'the way (they) treat staff' (para. 5.15) as this will be linked to core performance measures and 'to the financial resources they receive' (para. 5.15), for example through successful recruitment efforts and through providing educational opportunities. The Plan states that since February 1999 over 4000 nurses and midwives have returned to work in the NHS as a result of 'intensive action' (to recruit), suggesting that strategies to achieve high recruitment targets for the future are not envisaged as unrealistic.

The issue of recruitment and retention of nurses is at the heart of the Department of Health's human resources strategy. Bradshaw (1999) analysed several contributory factors to the nursing shortage: pay, job satisfaction, career structure, nursing's image, flexible working hours and education and training. He argues for a proper strategy to deal with 'poor pay and conditions of service which discourages recruitment which produces overwork, stress and low job satisfaction in the existing workforce which leads to attrition'. His conclusion comes out in favour of

> robust human resources policies which: predict the numbers of nurses required, clarify their role within the overall skill mix, provide equal opportunities, include an equitable system of remuneration that recognises the skills of individual nurses, supports systematic staff development and sustains personal motivation.

Since the publication of the NHS Plan there have been several well-publicized measures to recruit more medical staff including 'a worldwide advertising campaign to recruit thousands of foreign doctors' (*The Times*, 20 August 2001). The UK is already facing a serious shortage of GPs, partly because thousands of Indian-trained doctors who were recruited in the 1970s are now beginning to retire. The NHS Plan appears committed to delivering 7500 more consultants and 2000 more GPs by the end of 2004 as the present government does not wish to renege continually on its promises to cut waiting lists.

Workforce issues play an important role in the publication *A Quality Strategy for Social Care* (DoH 2000b) which builds upon the earlier White Paper *Modernising Social Services: Promoting Independence, Improving Protection, Raising Standards* (DoH 1998). A key theme is of raising standards in the workplace, calling for a clear definition of the roles of staff, for staff objectives to be related to service objectives, for better supervision and management and for improved education and training (confessing that 80 per cent of social care employees in a workforce of around one million had no recognized qualifications). Both documents stress the need for 'broader workforce planning' but fail to offer solutions for tackling the problem of recruitment, training and career progression. The somewhat restricted strategic remit states that policies to combat poverty and social exclusion will create new roles for workers and, as a consequence, 'the social care workforce needs to be geared to this new environment'

(DoH 2000b: para. 97). A Social Care Institute for Excellence (SCIE) is proposed 'to make knowledge about what works a truly effective force in improving quality' and 'to draw together and disseminate what works best in social care, in order to ensure that social services are no longer a "postcode lottery"' (DoH 2000b: para. 30).

The strategy for social care promises high-quality staff, a new focus on workforce training and development and reform of social work education. The intention is for the government to work with the employer-based National Training Organisation for Personal Social Services (TOPSS) to develop occupational standards for the whole of the workforce. However, placing the prime responsibility for training with employers may send out messages of cost cutting, and curtailing opportunities for career progression, as employers will be allowed to put a price ceiling on employees. It may not hence be possible to provide appropriate career opportunities for those with advanced specialist skills in social care and social work. Whereas 'delivering excellence' may be a central government goal, retaining service delivery within a mixed public–private sector will fail by definition to guarantee equivalent standards in the workplace. Without regulation or fiat such standards are likely to diversify. This strategy for social care modernization appears to suggest a reinvention of the social work role, asserting that 'social workers will be working in a variety of settings'; hence a central activity should be upon forming partnerships:

> The profession will develop its ability to:
> - work with excluded people and restore them to mainstream services
> - assist people to identify problems and their solutions
> - balance the needs of individuals with the needs of their families and wider networks
> - work creatively with other professionals
> - identify conflict and negotiate solutions.
>
> (DoH 2000b: para. 101)

The strategy calls for a 'refocusing' and for a radical consideration of the future structure and content of social work training; and includes criticism that social work needs to be more evidence-based:

> Recent Social Services Inspectorate inspections have shown that social workers need to rediscover some of (their) core skills of assessment, so that decision-making and care-planning are based on a sound analysis and understanding of the person's unique personality, history and circumstances. Social workers' own skills need to be seen as a resource to be used and offered in the assessment.
>
> (DoH 2000b: para. 103)

Professionalism and partnership

Partnership has become the mantra of the 1997 Labour government in its efforts to reform public services – to break down 'old-fashioned demarcations between staff and barriers between services':

> The two White Papers, *Modernising Social Services* and *The New NHS: Modern, Dependable* set out new approaches to facilitate closer working between local agencies. In particular, Health Improvement Programmes and Health Action Zones provide the means for health and local authorities to work together with other independent bodies, as well as local communities and individuals, to pursue joint objectives to improve health and reduce inequalities.
>
> (DoH 1999, para. 10)

The government's emphasis on finding 'joined-up' solutions to social problems has triggered varied rhetoric on partnership. The policy agenda for tackling social exclusion and regenerating communities (Social Exclusion Unit 1998), and key developments intended to improve matters for children and families such as Education Action Zones, Health Action Zones, Sure Start and Healthy Living Centres, require partnership at professional and grassroots delivery level. Inherent is the notion of professionals working together cooperatively and harmoniously, this activity 'rest(ing) on an implicit ideology of neutral, benevolent expertise in the service of consensual, self-evident values' (Challis *et al.* 1988: 17). There seems an assumption that consensual values, benevolence and mutual self-interest are implicitly compatible.

Inter-agency and interprofessional coordination and collaboration are not, however, readily achieved in practice (Sands *et al.* 1990; Hudson 1999a; Freeman *et al.* 2000; Easen *et al.* 2000) and further research is needed regarding outcomes and costs (Schmitt 2001). The three most frequent reasons for failures in collaboration drawn from research are cited as being differing professional perspectives on problems, different occupational cultures and confusion over professional roles (Sweeney *et al.* 2000). The cultures and histories of social work and nursing, for instance, are distinctly different, and this will have an effect on values, priorities and models of working (Beattie 1995). There is evidence of differences in moral priorities and values between the two professions, for instance in relation to family responsibilities and state involvement (Dalley 1993). Differences and similarities in professional values in relation to nursing and social work should perhaps be accepted as unavoidable and even desirable, and there may be good arguments for concentrating on optimizing the quality of interprofessional dialogue around values, rather than for seeking to remove those differences (Wilmot 1995).

Challenges for inter-agency work in the child protection field with the shift to a more needs-led approach have been explored (Morrison 2000). The interrelationship of three domains of partnership is a key theme in managing this change: partnerships with service users, partnerships between agencies/disciplines, and partnership within agencies/disciplines. The importance of intra-agency clarity and commitment is highlighted. The emphasis from government on partnership within social care and health care agencies has tended to be on strategic inter-agency working rather than interprofessional relationships (Hudson 1999a). This, Hudson suggests, is a major imbalance, as it is front-line professionals and related staff who will have to deliver integrated care to service users. If their relationships are not clear and constructive, he suggests, broad inter-agency strategies may fail.

Collaboration itself is a complex phenomenon (Hennemann *et al.* 1995) and different models have been explored (Hudson 1999b). Different philosophies of team working can present difficulties for multi-professional teamwork (Freeman *et al.* 2000). Indicators for positive interprofessional teamworking appear to be the personal qualities and commitment of staff, communication within the team and the opportunity to develop creative working methods within the team (Molyneux 2001). Issues of 'personhood' cannot be ignored, as professional and disciplinary differences are manifested in terms of who professional persons consider themselves to be in relation to what is expected of them (Dombeck 1997). Territorial issues may arise out of concerns for personal integrity in doing one's work, and successful collaboration is enhanced by a process of cultural sensitization to other professional groups. When boundaries of distinct groups appear to come under threat from integration of various professional groups, there may be a sense of loss of professional identity, there may be tribalism or feelings of ambivalence, conflict and grief, and the need to maintain the self-confidence of different professional groups is very real (Atkins 1998).

How to establish motivation and momentum towards partnership has been a concern for health and social care sectors since the mid-1970s. Wistow and Whittingham (1988) diagnosed the original difficulty as couched within the simultaneous reorganizations of the NHS and local government which came into effect in 1974. Here the distribution of functions between the recognized services was based on a single fundamental principle: that their responsibilities should be demarcated according to the skills of providers rather than the needs of the individuals they served (DHSS 1970). Since the mid-1970s the Department of Health has urged both agency and professional collaboration but concurrently it has created administrative, organizational and professional obstacles to achieving a needs-based approach, for example in the case of community care (Malin *et al.* 1999: 16).

The problem with trying to create professional partnership, according to Sennett (1999: 84), is that it is based upon 'a domain of demeaning superficiality which besets the workplace'. Groups, teams, tend to hold together through keeping to the surface of things – shared superficiality keeps people together by avoiding difficult, divisive, personal questions. Hunter (2000) alleges that it is the absence of authority (or rather the 'leader' figure) which mars successful partnership and that this is prerequisite to delivering agreed objectives; also that

> deep, lasting partnerships can only be established where there are stable long-term relationships and real trust can emerge ... all the pressures associated with short-term deadlines, and the demand for instant results, militate against such partnerships being given a fair wind.
>
> (Hunter 2000: 524)

Writers who have considered twin concepts of partnership and collaboration tend to conclude that it is the fault of organizational systems failing to make it happen and claim that professional practice roots create a barrier. The development of a primary care-led NHS, promoted by the 1997 Labour government and set to continue during Labour's second term in office (Labour Party 2001), has led to a significant reappraisal of working practices and a renewed emphasis on collaboration and 'teamwork' between health and social care professionals. Changes in patterns of health care delivery and in the structure of the NHS itself have impacted upon the direction of the health professions towards different styles of partnership working (see, for example, Biggs 1993: 151; Poulton and West 1993: 918–20; Shaw 1993: 256–62; Leathard 1994: 7–23; Hugman 1995: 31–45; Mackay *et al.* 1995: 5–10). The focus has shifted from the 'specific combination of skills, knowledge and values' (Hugman 1995: 41) that characterize any single health or social care profession to how effective professionals can be in operating across boundaries and deploying skills entrepreneurially – many of which are complementary or overlapping – in order to achieve better outcomes, for example promotion of effective and individualized patient care.

The debate over the value of multidisciplinary education, which began around the early 1990s, has complemented this development towards modes of professional partnership, responding to the changing environment of the NHS despite criticism of lack of 'hard' evidence supporting outcomes of multiprofessional education *per se* (Pirrie 1998). It has been thought of as one way of equipping professionals to provide a 'seamless' service, albeit delivered by health and social care professionals maintaining their discrete professional identities. Very little of current provision of multiprofessional education in universities has addressed interprofessional issues as the higher education agenda promotes a pattern of multiprofessional education in which content was chosen because it was defined as 'common' across different professions (Miller *et al.* 1999). In the specific case of community care provision, the Department of Health advocated inter-agency training, 'particularly where staff from the Health Service, Social Services and other agencies need to work collaboratively and acquire similar or complementary skills' (DoH 1991b: para. 1.20). The example of learning disability nursing illustrates not only the requirement to change the nursing role but to develop a 'capacity to work as an integral member of a team' (DoH 1996). The Department of Health's *Caring for People* White Paper (1989a) and the 1990 National Health Service and Community Care Act both promoted joint planning and working between the various agencies involved in the delivery of services. Research commissioned by the English National Board for Nursing, Midwifery and Health Visiting (ENB) on mental health and learning disability nursing during the 1990s has indicated that nurses need interprofessional and multidisciplinary teamworking skills, to be proactive in coordinating multiprofessional services and to create effective multi-agency working across statutory and voluntary sectors (Redfern *et al.* 1996; Nolan *et al.* 1997; Alaszewski *et al.* 2001; Long *et al.* 2001).

Summary

The first part of this chapter examines how welfare professionals have been subjected to increased managerial and political control, and how audit, regulation and appraisal have required that they become more accountable. The issue of caring professions being mediators between producers (the state) and consumers (patients and service users), that their activities are defined largely by the state, and the lack of clear definition of their output, are factors which have encroached on their autonomy and upon the scope and opportunity that they have for making independent judgements (the notion of 'indeterminacy'). There is a tension between the reflective practice aims of caring professions and their having been subjected to forms of deskilling – a conversion in perception and status – and fulfilling protocols and guidelines imposed by bureaucrats and managers. This produces an argument that this mode of inspected, regulated professionalism has questionably threatened the positive, creative aspects of professional practice. The promotion of consumer power may entail losses such as establishing more adversarial relations between professionals and service users than ways of constructive partnership, the promotion of which is an aim of the present Labour government.

The second part of this chapter traces the political attack on professions in health and social care during the 1980s and 1990s. This has been arguably a response to the absence of effective political and managerial control, lack of earlier accountability, absence of genuine 'voice' for users and an over-influence of professionals in the sphere of policy making. Recent government policies and government rhetoric have criticized welfare professions' expertise and ethic of service; their maintenance of standards; variations in practice, evidencing a slow uptake of new knowledge and practice among professionals; a high error rate; and the demonstration of unnecessary interprofessional rivalries.

The third part focuses upon New Labour policies (clinical governance, national service frameworks) to reduce service delivery inequalities, to improve standards, involve users to a greater degree and break down demarcations between staff and barriers between services – the 'modernization' protocol. Workforce issues are central to the NHS Plan (recruitment and retention of professionals) and to the social care agenda, both of which attempt to make professionals more accountable and more willing to accept scrutiny and transparency. This particular argument enmeshes a contemporary policy debate concerning sustainability of public services which, it is alleged, fail to address in adequate terms the matter of workforce planning and standards, recruitment or career development, despite this objective being a main feature of the political agenda for health and social welfare. There is an acknowledged low morale, motivation and commitment in public services and this is, most probably, due to poor resourcing, recurrent organizational restructurings and political changes in direction.

The final section addresses the issue of professionalism in the context of partnership as a means towards reform of public services. Differing professional perspectives on problems, different occupational cultures and confusion over professional roles would seem to have hampered partnerships and multidisciplinary working. Organizational loyalty, ways in which services are differently funded and, fundamentally, entrepreneurship – an outcome of managerialist culture – have impacted on individual professionals and sharpened disincentives to collaboration. Government has prioritized strategies for inter-agency rather than inter-professional working whereas the latter is perceived to be more important for the individual service user. Multidisciplinary education emerges in parallel but this is currently limited in scope and, from some available evidence, appears to fail to make strategic links with service activities.

References

Alaszewski, A., Gates, B., Motherby, E., Manthorpe, J. and Ayer, S. (2001) *Educational Preparation for Learning Disability Nursing: Outcomes Evaluation of the Contribution of Learning Disability Nurses within the Multi-professional, Multi-agency Team*, Research Highlights No. 47. London: English National Board for Nursing, Midwifery and Health Visiting.

Althaus, C. (1977) The application of agency theory to public sector management, in G. Davis, B. Sullivan and A. Yeatman (eds) *The New Contractualism?*, pp. 137–53. Nathan: Centre for Australian Public Sector Management, Griffith University.

Atkins, J. (1998) Tribalism, loss and grief: issues for multiprofessional education, *Journal of Interprofessional Care*, 12 (3): 303–7.

Aucoin, P. (1990) Administrative reform in public management: paradigms, principles, paradoxes and pendulums, *Governance*, 3: 115–37.

Bartlett, W., Roberts, J. and Le Grand, J. (eds) (1998) *A Revolution in Social Policy: Quasi-market Reforms in the 1990s.* Bristol: The Policy Press.

Beattie, A. (1995) War and peace among the health tribes, in K. Soothill, L. Mackay and C. Webb (eds) *Interprofessional Relations in Heath Care.* London: Edward Arnold.

Biggs, S. (1993) User participation and interprofessional collaboration in community care, *Journal of Interprofessional Care*, 7: 151–9.

Boston, J., Martin, J., Pallot, J. and Walsh, P. (1996) *Public Management: The New Zealand Model.* Oxford: Oxford University Press.

Bradshaw, P. (1999) A service in crisis? Reflections on the shortage of nurses in the British National Health Service, *Journal of Nursing Management*, 7: 129–32.

Bryson, J. and Smith-Ring, P. (1990) A transaction-based approach to policy intervention, *Policy Studies*, 23: 205–29.

Buxton, M. *et al.* (1985) *Costs and Benefits of Heart Transplant Programmes.* London: HMSO.

Calnan, M. and Williams, S. (1995) Challenges to professional autonomy in the United Kingdom? The perceptions of general practitioners, *International Journal of Health Services*, 25 (2): 332–45.

Carr-Saunders, A. and Wilson, P. (1962) *The Professions.* Oxford: Clarendon Press.

Challis, L., Fuller, S., Henwood, M. *et al.* (1988) *Joint Approaches to Social Policy: Rationality and Practice.* Cambridge: Cambridge University Press.

Clarke, J. and Newman, J. (1993) Managing to survive: dilemmas of changing organisational forms in the public sector, in N. Deakin and R. Page (eds) *The Costs of Welfare.* Aldershot: Avebury.

Clarke, J. and Newman, J. (1997) *The Managerial State.* London: Sage Publications.

Dalley, G. (1993) Professional ideology or organisational tribalism? The health service–social work divide, in J. Walmesley (ed.) *Health, Welfare and Practice.* London: Sage Publications.

Dawes, R. (1994) *House of Cards: Psychology and Psychotherapy Built on Myth.* New York, NY: Free Press.

Deverall, K. and Sharma, V. (2000) Professionalism in everyday practice: issues of trust, experience and boundaries, in N. Malin (ed.) *Professionalism, Boundaries and the Workplace*, pp. 25–46. London: Routledge.

DHSS (Department of Health and Social Security) (1970) *National Health Service: The Future Structure of the NHS.* London: HMSO.

DoH (Department of Health) (1989a) *Caring for People: Community Care in the Next Decade and Beyond*, Cm 849. London: HMSO.

DoH (Department of Health) (1989b) *Working For Patients*, Cm 555. London: HMSO.

DoH (Department of Health) (1991a) *The Patient's Charter*. London: HMSO.

DoH (Department of Health) (1991b) *Community Care in the Next Decade and Beyond: Policy Guidance*. London: HMSO.

DoH (Department of Health) (1996) *Continuing the Commitment: The Report of the Learning Disability Project*. London: HMSO.

DoH (Department of Health) (1997) *The New NHS: Modern, Dependable*, Cm 3807. London: HMSO.

DoH (Department of Health) (1998) *Modernising Social Services: Promoting Independence, Improving Protection, Raising Standards*. London: HMSO.

DoH (Department of Health) (1999) *Saving Lives: Our Healthier Nation White Paper and Reducing Health Inequalities: An Action Report*, Health Service Circular/Local Authority Circular, HSC 1999/152: LAC (99) 26. London: HMSO.

DoH (Department of Health) (2000a) *The NHS Plan – a Plan for Investment, a Plan for Reform*, Cm 4818–1. London: HMSO.

DoH (Department of Health) (2000b) *A Quality Strategy for Social Care*, London: HMSO.

Dombeck, M. (1997) Professional personhood: training, territoriality and tolerance, *Journal of Interpersonal Care*, II (1): 9–21.

Easen, P., Atkins, M. and Dyson, A. (2000) Inter-professional collaboration and conceptualisations of practice, *Children and Society*, 14: 355–67.

Etzioni, A. (1969) *The Semi-professions and their Organisation: Teachers, Nurses and Social Workers*. New York, NY: Free Press.

Fish, D. and Coles, C. (2000) Seeing anew: understanding professional practice as artistry, in C. Davies, L. Finlay and A. Bullman (eds) *Changing Practice in Health and Social Care*, pp. 290–9. London: Sage Publications.

Flexner, A. ([1915] 2001) Is social work a profession?, *Research on Social Work Practice*, II (2), March: 152–65.

Foster, P. and Wilding, P. (2000) Whither welfare professionalism? *Social Policy and Administration*, 34 (2), June: 143–59.

Freeman, M., Miller, C. and Ross, N. (2000) The impact of individual philosophies of teamwork on multi-professional practice and the implications for education, *Journal of Interpersonal Care*, 14 (3): 237–47.

Gambrill, E. (1999) Evidence-based practice: an alternative to authority-based practice, *Families in Society*, 80: 341–50.

Gambrill, E. (2000) Social work: an authority-based profession, *Research on Social Work Practice*, II (2), March: 166–75.

Gladstone, D. (ed.) (2000) *Regulating Doctors*. London: Institute for the Study of Civil Society.

Glendinning, C. (1998) From general practice to primary care: developments in primary health care services 1990–1998, in E. Brunsdon *et al. Social Policy Review 10*. London: Social Policy Association.

Greenwood, E. (1957) Attributes of a profession, *Social Work*, 2 (3): 44–55.

Gregory, R. (1995) Accountability, responsibility and corruption: managing the 'public production process', in J. Boston (ed.) *The State under Contract*, pp. 56–77. Wellington: Bridget Williams Books.

Griffiths, Sir Roy (1983) *NHS Management Inquiry*. London: HMSO.

Griffiths, Sir Roy (1988) *Community Care: Agenda For Action*. London: HMSO.

Harrison, S., Hunter, D. and Pollitt, C. (1990) *The Dynamics of British Health Policy*. London: Unwin Hyman.

Harrison, S. and Pollitt, C. (1994) *Controlling Health Professionals*. Buckingham: Open University Press.

Hennemann, E., Lee, J. and Cohen, J. (1995) Collaboration: a concept analysis, *Journal of Advanced Nursing*, 21: 103–9

Hood, C. (1991) A public management for all seasons, *Public Administration*, 69: 3–19.

Hood, C. and Jackson, M. (1992) The new public management: a recipe for disaster?, in D. Parker and J. Handmer (eds) *Hazard Management and Emergency Planning: Perspectives on Britain*. London: James and James Science Publications.

Howe, D. (1986) *Social Workers and their Practice in Welfare Bureaucracies*. Aldershot: Gower.

Hudson, B. (1999a) Primary health care and social care: working across professional boundaries, Pt. 1: The changing context of inter-professional relationships, *Managing Community Care*, 7 (1): 15–22.

Hudson, B. (1999b) Primary health care and social care: working across professional boundaries, Pt. 2: Models of inter-professional collaboration, *Managing Community Care*, 7 (2): 15–20.

Hugman, R. (1991) *Power in Caring Professions*. Basingstoke: Macmillan.

Hugman, R. (1995) Contested territory and community services: interprofessional boundaries in health and social care, in K. Soothill, L. Mackay and C. Webb (eds) *Interprofessional Relations in Health Care*. London: Edward Arnold.

Hunter, D. (2000) Pitfalls of arranged marriages, *Health Service Journal*, 23 November, 22–3.

Johnson, T. (1972) *Professions and Power*. London: Macmillan.

Johnson, T. (1982) The state and the professions: peculiarities of the British, in A. Giddens and G. Mackenzie (eds) *Social Class and the Division of Labour*. Cambridge: Cambridge University Press.

Kassirer, J. (1993) Medicine at centre stage, *New England Journal of Medicine*, 328 (17): 1268.

Kettl, D. (1993) *Sharing Power: Public Governance and Private Markets*. Washington, DC: Brookings Institution.

Klein, R. (2001) *The New Politics of the NHS*, 4th edn. Harlow: Pearson Education.

Labour Party (2001) *Ambitions for Britain: New Labour, New Britain*. Labour manifesto.

Larkin, G. (1983) *Occupational Monopoly and Modern Medicine*. London: Tavistock Press.

Leape, L. (1994) Error in medicine, *Journal of the American Medical Association*, 272 (23): 1851.

Leathard, A. (ed.) (1994) *Going Inter-professional: Working Together for Health and Welfare*. London: Routledge.

Le Grand, J. and Bartlett, W. (1993) *Quasi-markets and Social Policy*. London: Macmillan.

Levi, M. (1998) *Of Rule and Revenue*. Berkeley, CA: University of California Press.

Long, A., Ryan, J. and Berry, J. (2001) *Exploring the Role and Contribution of the Nurse in the Multi-professional Rehabilitation Team*, Research Highlights No. 45. London: English National Board for Nursing, Midwifery and Health Visiting.

Macdonald, K. (1995) *The Sociology of the Professions*. London: Sage.

Mackay, L. (1990) Nursing: Just another job?, in P. Abbott and C. Wallace (eds) *The Sociology of the Caring Professions*. London: Falmer Press.

Mackay, L., Soothill, K. and Webb, C. (1995) Troubled times: the context for interprofessional collaboration?, in K. Soothill *et al.* (eds) *Interprofessional Relations in Health Care*. London: Edward Arnold.

Malin, N., Manthorpe, J., Race, D. and Wilmot, S. (1999) *Community Care for Nurses and the Caring Professions*. Buckingham: Open University Press.

Merkle, J. (1980) *Management and Ideology: The Legacy of the International Scientific Management Movement*, Berkeley, CA: UCL Press.

Miller, C. *et al.* (1999) The role of collaborative/shared learning in pre- and post-registration education in nursing, midwifery and health visiting, *ENB Reports*, No. 39, London: ENB.

Mintzberg, L. (1983) *Structure in Fives: Designing Organisational Effectiveness*. London: Prentice-Hall.

Molyneux, J. (2001) Interprofessional teamworking: what makes teams work well?, *Journal of Interprofessional Care*, 15 (1): 29–35.

Morrison, T. (2000) Working together to safeguard children: challenges and changes for inter-agency co-ordination in child protection, *Journal of Interprofessional Care*, 14 (4): 363–73.

Newble, D., Jolly, B. and Wakeford, R. (1994) 'Background', in D. Newble, B. Jolly and R. Wakeford (eds) *Certification and Recertification of Doctors: Issues in the Assessment of Clinical Competence*. Cambridge: Cambridge University Press.

Nolan, M., Booth, A., Nolan, J. and Mason, H. (1997) *Preparation for Multi-professional/Multi-agency Health Care Practice: The Nursing Contribution to Rehabilitation Within the Multi-disciplinary Team, Literature Review and Curric-ulum Analysis*, Research Highlights No. 28. London: English National Board for Nursing, Midwifery and Health Visiting.

North, D. (1990) *Institutions, Institutional Change and Economic Performance*. Cam-bridge: Cambridge University Press.

Perrow, C. (1979) *Complex Organisations: A Critical Essay*. New York, NY: Random House.

Pirrie, A. (1998) Rocky mountains and tired Indians: on territories and tribes. Reflections on multidisciplinary education in the health professions, *British Educational Research Journal*, 25 (1): 113–26.

Pollitt, C. (1993) The development of management thought, in M. Hill (ed.) *The Policy Process: A Reader*, pp. 299–312. Hemel Hempstead: Harvester.

Poulton, B. and West, M. (1993) Effective multi-disciplinary teamwork in primary health care, *Journal of Advanced Nursing*, 18: 918–25.

Ramia, G. and Carney, T. (2001) Contractualism, managerialism and welfare: the Australian experiment with a marketised employment services network, *Policy and Politics*, 29 (1): 59–80.

Redfern, S., Norman, I., Bodley, D., Holroyd, S. and White, E. (1996) *The Chang-ing Educational Needs of Mental Health and Learning Disability Nurses*, Re-search Highlights No. 22. London: English National Board for Nursing, Midwifery and Health Visiting.

Reed, M. (1988) The problem of human agency in organisational analysis, *Organ-ization Studies*, 9 (1): 33–46.

Rhodes, R. (1997) *Understanding Governance*. Buckingham: Open University Press.

Rhodes, R. (1998) Different roads to unfamiliar places: UK experience in comparative perspective, *Australian Journal of Public Administration*, 57 (4): 19–31.

Sands, R., Stafford, J. and McClelland, M. (1990) 'I beg to differ': conflict in the interdisciplinary team, *Social Work in Health Care*, 14 (3): 55–72.

Schmitt, M. (2001) Collaboration improves the quality of care: methodological challenges and evidence from US health care research, *Journal of Interprofessional Care*, 15 (1): 47–66.

Self, P. (1972) *Administrative Theories and Politics*. London: Allen & Unwin.

Sennett, R. (1999) *The Corrosion of Character*. London: Norton.

Shaw, I. (1993) The politics of inter-professional training – lessons from learning disability, *Journal of Interprofessional Care*, 7: 255–62.

Simon, H. (1945) *Administrative Behaviour*, 2nd edn. New York: Englewood Cliffs.

Social Exclusion Unit (1998) *Bringing Britain Together: A National Strategy for Neighbourhood Renewal*, Cm 4045. London: The Stationery Office.

Southon, G. and Braithwaite, J. (2000) The end of professionalism?, in C. Davies, L. Finlay and A. Bullman (eds) *Changing Practice in Health and Social Care*, pp 300–7. London: Sage.

Sweeney, K., Stead, J. and Cosford, L. (2000) Evidence-based practice: can this help joint working?, *Managing Community Care*, 8 (5): 21–7.

Taylor, F. W. (1911) *Principles of Scientific Management*. New York, NY: McGraw Hill.

Toren, N. (1972) *Social Work: The Case of a Semi-profession*. London: Sage.

Wilmot, S. (1995) Professional values and inter-professional dialogue, *Journal of Interprofessional Care*, 19 (3): 257–66.

Wistow, G. and Whittingham, D. (1988) Policy and research into practice, in D. Stockford (ed.) *Integrating Care Systems: Practical Perspectives*. Harlow: Longman.

Witz, A. (1992) *Professions and Patriarchy*. London: Routledge.

chapter **seven**

COMMUNITY CARE AND FAMILY POLICY

In this chapter we turn to the private and public roles of the family, exploring concepts of care and caring. We shall focus on gender as the key to developing understandings of the complex relations between work, family life and social care. We start with a brief discussion of demographic changes which underpin much discussion of care and family policy.

Family forms

Much political attention, at a very general level, portrays demographic change negatively. Rather than celebrating major improvements in the health status and lifespan of the population, problems are perceived in respect of an ageing population.

Instead of welcoming control over fertility and improvements in child health, doom-laden pronouncements occur about the imbalance between active workers and dependent retirement populations. As Clarke (2001) has observed, we need to be sceptical about the construction of certain features of social life as problems and can usefully adopt a 'constructionist' rather than a 'realist perspective': that is, we can recognize that social problems are shaped by different interests or the power of social groups. In doing so we can consider the impact of different social and historical circumstances. We should also think about what is left out of social problems, as well as what is put in. Gender is one such element that can be quickly glossed over (as can ethnicity, geography and disability). When we talk, for example, about ageing populations these are predominantly female. When we talk of fertility this is largely in relationship to women's reproduction, and when we talk about work and retirement this can miss out 'domestic' work, care work and emotional labour, as well as failing to consider the part-time employment status of many women.

Changes in care and family policies therefore are linked to five main social trends:

- geographical movements;
- labour market changes;
- fertility and reproduction;
- changes in patterns of death, disease and disability;
- changes in family formations and partnerships.

None of these is new. One of the major contributions to and consequences of industrialization in the nineteenth century in much of England and other parts of the UK was the move of populations from rural, agricultural communities to new or growing urban centres or overseas emigration. Movement of populations today is more complex, with individuals and families moving into the UK for a variety of reasons, from asylum-seeking to tourism. With rural and urban communities, movements can be economic or lifestyle-oriented. Emigration continues, with new patterns of retirement overseas or lengthy winter months in the sun.

In terms of family and care policies any movement becomes seen as a potential problem as it risks breaking up established networks. While networks may be a term that is largely equated with individual family members or carers, the notion that networks are important underlies principles of community development, for example in encouraging healthy lifestyles, or in promoting reciprocal exchanges of care between neighbours, friends and social groupings – women in particular.

The other four main social trends identified above have impacted on women in ways which affect their roles as carers and mothers. The decline of heavy industry has both promoted male unemployment among those with skills that are seen as outdated and exposed women as possibly the sole wage earners in some poorer households. Combining mother, carer and breadwinner roles places immense demands on individuals and exposes the limits of social welfare policies which seek to encourage commitment to all these areas simultaneously. New industries and support services draw women into employment and may offer attractive alternatives to full-time domestic work. Caring for children or for relatives can be seen as an activity which women should be able to manage in the context of their employment. The notion of 'juggling' work and care in particular (Manthorpe and Phillips 1998) is a popular means of describing how individuals, rather than policy makers, see the activities involved in managing interconnections between home and work lives.

Fertility is an area which brings together technology, moral, emotional and economic equations. Whether there are too many children or too few, family policy sets out a range of interventions in the lives of individuals. At crude levels these can be the 'carrot and stick' of financial penalties and inducements. The decline in the birth rate in the UK, for example, was seen as a major problem by Beveridge and others in their early discussions of social insurance during the Second World War (Harris 1977: 390).

Family policy then can be seen as part of social welfare, and indeed there is little in social welfare that can be conceived as not impacting on families. However, as Manning has observed (1998), families are the focus of government concern and action while meeting most social needs. While some might take issue with his view that the modern family now provides 'less welfare' than previously because this generalizes a wide variety of experiences, this does not mean that government interest in the family has waned. Much government activity, regardless of the policy-making focus, is seen through and presented through the lens of how it impacts on families.

It is surprising then that family policy is only weakly coordinated and, at times, seems contradictory. Women, for example, are encouraged to be active parents, helping their children to read, their schools to flourish and their communities to fight street crime, transport excesses or pollution, and simultaneously face challenges to return to work in areas of severe staff shortages such as nursing, teaching or information technology. Millar (1998: 121) has commented: 'Family policy, it seems, is nothing and everything at the same time'.

We noted earlier that fertility and reproduction were areas of family life that had witnessed enormous changes – far beyond questions of the numbers of children and whether such numbers could be turned on or off like a tap to respond to calls for population increases or declines. As Millar has observed, current family life is varied and heterogeneous, though whether it was ever uniform is doubtful. Social problems associated with continual childbearing, such as the poor health of many mothers identified in the early years of the NHS, are now overtaken by the social problems raised by those who are unable to have children of their own. Childlessness, for a variety of other social factors, is now less easy to 'fix' by the adoption of other people's children. Childlessness, because of medical difficulties, can be something that demands NHS investment of resources. New assistive technologies may enable women to conceive in later years, or without the status of marriage or partnership. While 'smaller families' are thus generally seen as the product of such control over fertility, the number of children in a family unit is only one factor in the evolution of different family models.

In a multi-ethnic Britain, variations are evident in family forms but so too are continuities and commonalities. Ahmad (1996) has pointed to the role of 'family-based obligations in migration and settlement' (p. 51) and how these evolve over time and within the context of second generations. He argued that there are many factors at work building up patterns of family obligation in some ethnic minority families but that these are negotiated, and thus liable to change, rather than firmly set.

Such complexities make assessment of individuals and families complicated, since many people do not live in predictable formulations. The use of family trees which allows people to sketch out some important links and relationships is a helpful way of seeing individual families in all their complexity. Concepts such as the 'reconstituted' family, formed through remarriage and step-parenthood, can be made more concrete. Ideas about 'vertical' families, where links are important between generations such as grandparents, parents and children, can also convey particular family patterns.

Changes in patterns of death, disease and disability have likewise affected family life and ideas about who belongs and is entitled to the status of family membership. Disability has been one factor, for example, strongly affecting a person's membership of a family. Having a disability could mean that the forces of welfare could remove a person from their family, through, for instance, the certification and removal of a person with mental disability to an asylum or long-stay hospital. Mental health problems have also been implicated in the extent to which social systems affect individuals' experience of family life. Prior (1999) has drawn attention to the ways in which women were admitted to psychiatric hospitals for a variety of reasons: 'The images of female madness provided the justification for the imposition of treatments sometimes for the woman's benefit, always for the benefit of her immediate family and sometimes for the benefit of the therapist' (1999: 79). As she has observed, detailed analysis of admissions to psychiatric hospitals in Ireland points to the importance of financial considerations within families and farming and the social consequences of admission rather than the severity of a person's symptoms (1999: 55). Such discussion draws on two major ideas about mental illness: theories of

- social causation: mental distress is the result of stresses or conflict between social roles and lived experiences;
- social construction: mental illness or distress is the product of patriarchal oppression of women and its coercion of them into stereotypical female identities.

(See Prior 1999: 78)

Over time, changes in patterns of disability or illness may affect family life and vice versa. The stresses for women of living in violent relationships or abusive families, for example, may be ameliorated by a social system which allows a woman divorce or separation, does not stigmatize her or her children and enables her to build up self-esteem and to avoid depression, trauma or injury.

The final social trend, changes in family formations and partnerships, is central to what we understand by care. Demographic changes within this trend, however, include a wide range of items, some more welcomed by government than others. Many of them are intricately linked to the other trends already identified. Very few of them are entirely new. The Beveridge Committee, in respect of the social insurance needs of women, for example, identified the special problems of 'unmarried wives' who today might be viewed as cohabiting, of 'deserted' mothers, today's single parents and 'domestic spinsters' who today might be seen as full-time carers for their parents (Harris 1977: 395).

Thus, despite rises in the divorce rate and growing numbers of single parent households, such family forms are not new. For women, the concept of dependence is a continual theme. As Lewis has argued (1998: 89), governments have generally assumed that women depend on male breadwinners. In return, women undertake key social roles in respect of motherhood, childrearing, domestic work and care for sick or disabled family members. Within such a model of gendered dependency, women's wages are not central to the family's essential well-being and so women can work part-time or cease work or restart work according to demands on their household and family time. Collective provision, either in the form of pre-school child care, school holiday provision or good quality support services for family members with special needs for care or assistance, is not a priority. Lewis used lone mothers (Beveridge's deserted mothers) to illustrate the ways in which social policies have treated women as mothers until comparatively recently. At times of unemployment and consensus about the valued role of mothers, governments have seen it appropriate for motherhood to negate unemployment. Women looking after children were seen to be engaged in valued activity, could receive income support and were not required to register as unemployed. The 1990s, however, have seen moves away from this blanket categorization: '. . . the pendulum has been swinging back towards treating lone mothers more as workers, and in Britain towards forcing men to maintain their biological children' (Lewis 1998: 89).

Women, particularly single mothers who have no male breadwinner to depend on, are increasingly seen to be over-reliant on the state and to provide inadequate role models to other women and their own children. The creation of teenage single mothers as a particular category, symbolic of dependency on the state, provides another example of how family formation is important in thinking around the interrelations between gender and care. Teenage pregnancy was the subject of one of the earliest Social Exclusion Unit's reports (1999), a subject that Beveridge, with his concern about the declining birth rate and the generally lower average

age for marriage and conception, might not have been particularly worried about. For him, the problem of poverty and the question of how best to support poor children, such as those from large families, was to underpin the development of social insurance and the welfare state. (See also Chapter 2 in this respect.)

The control of teenage pregnancy has been seen as symbolic in tackling a dependency culture. Unlike 'deserted mothers' or widows, the position of such women is tinged by morality. It may be helpful to see teenage mothers as creating particular challenges to dependency stereotypes. They are in a 'limbo' position, no longer dependent as daughters on their own families or fathers; they are in disadvantageous positions economically when young people's wages are low (despite the minimum wage); they are unable to depend financially and, as is often portrayed, emotionally or practically on the (teenage) fathers of their children. Teenage mothers, and increasingly single mothers, are women whose roles as mothers or employees are debated at policy levels to resolve contradictions between supporting family life and ideas that such support weakens families' abilities to look after themselves. This tension was particularly evident during the period of Conservative government from 1988 to 1997. Glennerster (2000) observed a variety of measures undertaken to withdraw state support to families in certain circumstances or categories:

- the withdrawal of income support for 16- to 18-year-olds;
- reduced benefits for 18- to 25-year-olds;
- the Child Support Act to assert parental responsibilities (especially fathers);
- introduction of student loans;
- parental responsibilities for a child's 'crimes'.

(Glennerster 2000: 197)

Such moves challenged ideas about a sharp break between adult and child status. They indicated that parental responsibility extends beyond child care. In such ways notions develop that the state is taking over family commitments. Despite major changes in some family formations, themes of responsibilities and dependence/independence endure, and as we have seen, these impact upon women in particular. The Child Support Act 1991, for example, while seemingly directed at men (the 'absent' partners of teenage mothers, those responsible for deserted mothers, to sum up the stereotypical prejudices) impacted upon women by requiring them to provide details of their former partners. As Barnes and Prior (2000) noted:

One particular aspect of the Act which has caused considerable anger and distress is the benefit penalty imposed on the 'parents with care' (who are usually mothers) if they withhold information about the absent parent from whom payment is required. Women have been faced with choices of losing benefits or risking consequences of the anger of their ex-partners unwilling or unable to make payments.

(Barnes and Prior 2000: 88)

Pragmatism or direction?

The illustrations above of social trends and their particular relevance to social policies affecting women demonstrate how social problems associated with the family and with women draw governments into political minefields. The Child Support Act 1991, for example, constructed a bureaucratic, rule-oriented system seeking fairness and impartiality. This has proved difficult to implement, evoking public protest, media criticism and subsequent revisions, each seemingly making the system increasingly complex. The Child Support Act 1995, in attempting to meet such criticism, provoked further concerns that the system was unfair or simply fundamentally flawed.

Government action in private family life has often proved difficult and cautious policy makers have noted the problem of acting on morality. For women, this unwillingness to intervene in family life or to alter patterns of dependence by moving them from dependence on male partners to dependence on the workplace helps to explain the enduring legacy of much social security and pension provision. The deliberations of the Beveridge Committee, over half a century ago in the early years of the Second World War, 'raised many fundamental questions about contemporary social structure and women's rights' (Harris 1977: 403). The Committee's attempts to categorize women by reference to their family status (widows, mothers, wives, spinsters and so on) and to see motherhood and marriage as occupations as well as moral investments made the insurance position of women complex. Over the decades, continual changes to the social security system had to be made to respond to the inadequacies of seeing women in 'categories' which were relatively static. While Britain, for example, has very high rates of marriage, most women are now in employment.

Treading carefully through the political minefield of family life, many governments might choose to leave this area alone. Labour's Third Way might be seen as an attempt to avoid extremes of the Old Left and New Right (Powell 2000: 47) by its emphasis on rights accompanied by responsibilities:

From the perspective of gender equity, the model pursued is primarily a 'universal breadwinner model', in which the breadwinner role is universalised so that women can be citizen-workers alongside men, as opposed to the 'care-giver parity' or 'universal care-giver' models which respectively support informal care work and encourage men to combine caring and paid work in the same way that women currently do.

(Powell 2000: 48–9)

Such an approach, however, requires forms of compulsion which are always likely to be unpopular. The social trends identified in this section provide numerous examples of how apparently simple policies to encourage or prevent certain trends have difficulties in implementation. In the next section we shall consider one aspect of gender and family functioning in more detail: the area which has come to be seen as informal care.

Informal care – the housewives' lot?

The earlier section noted Beveridge's concern for 'domestic spinsters' caring for their elderly parents whose own lives in old age were likely to be in poverty. The altruism of such women was seen as common to their sex: 'Serving, exhausting oneself without thought of personal reward – isn't that what most women do most of their lives in peace or war?' (Beveridge 1942: 38). Such ideas have been examined by feminists to explore whether women are, by nature, more willing or better able to be carers or whether such a position serves the interests of men, the state and the economy. Gilligan, for example, asked whether care was natural to women, noting: 'Women's place in man's life cycle has been that of nurturer, caretaker and helpmate, the weaver of these relationships on which she in turn relies' (1982: 17). Her view that women were differentiated from men by a feminine ethic of care emphasized that this might be in men's interests but it could also be a way of establishing identity for women and a source of common supportive experiences.

Such debates link together caring for disabled adults and also children. There has been less interest in recent years on the links between child care and caring for adults, possibly because to place the two together suggests that disabled people are infantilized. Nonetheless, there are a number of common themes – not the least being the use of the word care in both contexts. Some disability writers, such as Shakespeare (2000), have argued that the term care is inappropriate ansd should be replaced by support.

Common themes between child care and care/support for disabled adults include:

- an emphasis on the family and/or home as being the best possible environment;
- suggestions that women are best suited to such activity;

- the acceptance that both activities do not require training or prior experience;
- professional support being available on an advisory basis or in a crisis;
- the market place of support services (playgroups, nurseries, day care);
- the stress on carers/mothers;
- the pleasures and satisfactions in such roles;
- the regulation of some support services to instil trust and to avoid exploitation;
- the financial costs of both activities;
- limited replacement of foregone income through carers' benefits or child benefit.

One way of moving such general points to the particular is to consider research studies which focus on individual examples of caring. Drawing on a biographical approach which encouraged carers to set their experiences in personal, local and political contexts, Chamberlayne and King (2000) considered three examples of how carers live with their responsibilities. Possibly not surprisingly, their examples of carers who embraced their new social identities and were proactive in making social contacts were both men. The authors found that Mr Allahm and Mr Merton participated in a range of social circles, some associated with caring and disability campaigning. They had moved from the private to public sphere.

A second type of carer experience identified by Chamberlayne and King was one where carers turned to other family members for support, at times because services were inadequate. This did not mean a lack of outside contact, but more emphasis on the family. The third type of carers identified were reluctantly moving to accept formal support, typically thinking about a move for the disabled person out of the family home. This transitional period was seen to be stressful or unhappy in some cases.

Chamberlayne and King make the point that caring can be flexible and adaptive. Over time carers adjust and respond to events or circumstances. Indeed, they noted that British carers had to be adaptive as services seem to be continually changing. As they observed, carers were aware of restrictions to formal services and the dilemma, for many, of knowing that residential services might be more available than supportive and sufficient community-based services.

The inadequacy of community care services places carers in a difficult position. Twigg and Atkin (1993) considered the 'ambiguous' position of carers, noting that they were part of agencies' concerns yet were not clients or service users. Professionals, they considered, could see carers either as helpful assistive resources; some as co-workers, such was their level of expertise; some as co-clients with their own poor health or needs for support; and some as 'superseded' carers who needed professional support or encouragement to 'let go' of their caring tasks to provide greater independence for the disabled person. Not unexpectedly, many carers do not always share such perceptions.

The 1990s were a decade in which a series of studies of carers and a number of reports and accounts from carers themselves brought informal care directly into the political limelight. The Carers' National Strategy (Her Majesty's Government 1999) established that there was public acceptance, in theory at least, of three key principles. Carers should be able to:

- take up caring or not;
- receive help and support at various stages;
- care without severe costs to their own health, social or economic positions.

Choice is a key theme and one which represents a major sea change in former statements which have stressed the bonds of care, as exemplified by the White Paper *Growing Older* (DHSS 1981): '. . . the primary sources of support and care for elderly people are informal and voluntary. These spring from the personal ties of friendship and neighbourhood. They are irreplaceable' (para. 19). As we identified in Chapter 4, choice is a key concept in current social policy. Both service users and carers are to have choice, as the extension of direct payments and carers' vouchers under the Family and Disabled Children Act 2000 signifies.

Choice for carers may be seen as part of consumer behaviour and is a response to critiques of services as being inflexible and ill-equipped to respond sensitively to individual needs. In line with consumerism, choice is also related to information and education among its consumers. One key arena where carer choice may conflict with user choice lies in provision for people with mental health problems. The influential series of public inquiries into homicide involving users of mental health services has drawn attention to the rights of people with mental health problems to privacy and confidentiality when set beside what families consider to be their rights to information, particularly if they are providing the care in the community (Stanley and Manthorpe 2001), at times at considerable cost to themselves.

Informal care, like parenthood, may be portrayed as a matter of choice, or lifestyle option. Research, however, suggests that many carers have few options and that caring is often not a matter of informed choice. Nolan *et al.* (2001), for example, have argued that relatives of older people in hospital are often unprepared for their caring role and that they acquire their skills and expertise haphazardly. Hospital discharge, despite its repeated identification as a time when preparation would be beneficial, appears to remain uncoordinated and disempowering. Few opportunities to exercise choice are possible in the haste to 'unblock' hospital beds.

Arguments that practitioners, in either hospital, community health or social services settings, equally lack power to halt the march of rapid hospital discharge can further confirm carers' doubts that there are any alternatives than their care. While many men are involved, particularly older spouses, in the provision of such support, it is most likely to be women who are conceived as carers. The next section focuses on the economic costs of such support.

The notion of the costs of caring has been steadily built up by evidence from studies of various carers and their families. Glendinning (1992), for example, noted family carers frequently had to pay for

- one-off capital costs – for example, washing machines;
- aids and adaptations – such as bathroom furniture;
- regular household expenditure – higher heating bills for example,

and often had to lose out on current earnings or future income.

Such costs are often borne by women. It is they who are more likely to give up employment, to work part-time or to forego opportunities. These indicators apply to mothers, but also to women caring for other family members. Even in respect of later life, Wright's research (2000) has identified ways in which former carers continue to suffer the financial consequences of an older person's admission to care in a nursing or residential home. Despite having 'saved' the state significant sums through their caring work, such former carers could be:

- liable to pay part of their joint income/savings in contributing to care costs;
- subject to variations or inaccuracies in local authority calculations;
- under pressure to make up necessary charges in order to arrange a home suitable for their relative;
- asked or expected to meet extra costs imposed by a home;
- meeting the costs of visiting;
- losing a future inheritance.

Women may be particularly disadvantaged by any or all of these factors. They are likely, in any event, to have shouldered considerable caring responsibilities before agreeing to residential or nursing home care.

Conclusion

This chapter has explored the private lives of family carers in respect of policy issues raised by considering this area of life which potentially affects us all – now or in the future. Families, their shape, size, behaviour and norms, are central to social policy. They are not passive, however, nor homogeneous, but vary and adapt to changing circumstances. A Britain which is increasingly multi-ethnic may expect this variety to be enhanced.

References

Ahmad, W. I. U. (1996) Family obligations and social change among Asian communities, in W. I. U. Ahmad and K. Atkin (eds) *'Race' and Community Care*, pp. 51–72. Buckingham: Open University Press.

Barnes, M. and Prior, D. (2000) *Private Lives as Public Policy*. Birmingham: Venture Press.

Beveridge, W. (1942) *The Pillars of Social Security*. London: George Allen and Unwin.

Chamberlayne, P. and King, A. (2000) *Cultures of Care: Biographies of Carers in Britain and the Two Germanies*. Bristol: The Policy Press.

Clarke, J. (2001) Social problems: sociological perspectives, in M. May, R. Page and E. Brinsdon (eds) *Understanding Social Problems: Issues in Social Policy*. Oxford: Blackwell.

DHSS (Department of Health and Social Security) (1981) *Growing Older*, Cmnd 8173. London: HMSO.

Gilligan, C. (1982) *In a Different Voice*. Cambridge, MA: Harvard University Press.

Glendinning, C. (1992) *The Costs of Informal Care*. London: HMSO.

Glennerster, H. (2000) *British Social Policy Since 1945*, 2nd edn. Oxford: Blackwell.

Harris, J. (1977) *William Beveridge: A Biography*. Oxford: Oxford University Press.

Her Majesty's Government (1999) *Caring About Carers: A National Strategy for Carers*. London: The Stationery Office.

Lewis, J. (1998) Feminist perspectives, in P. Alcock, A. Erskine and M. May (eds) *The Student's Companion to Social Policy*, pp. 85–90. Oxford: Blackwell.

Manning, N. (1998) Social needs, social problems and social welfare, in P. Alcock, A. Erskine and M. May (eds) *The Student's Companion to Social Policy*, pp. 31–6. Oxford: Blackwell.

Manthorpe, J. and Phillips, J. (1998) Working carers – people who juggle both roles, *Practice* 10 (2), 37–48.

Millar, J. (1998) Social policy and family policy, in P. Alcock, A. Erskine and M. May (eds) *The Student's Companion to Social Policy*, pp. 121–7. Oxford: Blackwell.

Nolan, M., Davies, S. and Grant, G. (eds) (2001) *Working with Older People and their Families*. Buckingham: Open University Press.

Powell, M. (2000) New Labour and the Third Way in the British welfare state: a new and distinctive approach? *Critical Social Policy*, 20 (1): 39–60.

Prior, P. M. (1999) *Gender and Mental Health*. London: Macmillan.

Shakespeare, T. (2000) *Help*. Birmingham: Venture Press.

Social Exclusion Unit (1999) *Teenage Pregnancy*, Cm. 4342. London: The Stationery Office.

Stanley, N. and Manthorpe, J. (2001) Reading mental health inquiries: messages for social work, *Journal of Social Work*, 1 (1): 77–99.

Twigg, J. and Atkin, K. (1993) *Carers Perceived*. Buckingham: Open University Press.

Wright, F. (2000) Continuing to pay: the consequences for family caregivers of an older person's admission to a care home, *Social Policy and Administration*, 34 (2): 191–205.

chapter **eight**

EVALUATING SERVICES: QUALITY ASSURANCE AND THE QUALITY DEBATE

Introduction

Quality assurance is, as Alazewski and Manthorpe (1993) point out, a phenomenon of its time. It is no accident that it emerged as a concept in the middle decades of the twentieth century, and became a key concept in health and social care in the last two decades of the century. Alazewski and Manthorpe identify it as a post-Fordist phenomenon, the product of an increasingly fragmented and individualized relationship between consumer and producer. Fordism, named after the US industrialist Henry Ford, worked on the principle, articulated by Navarro (1994), that 'mass production requires mass consumption' (pp. 136–7). In the Fordist situation goods and services were mass produced and relatively undifferentiated, and the consumer was perceived as having a standardized and predictable set of requirements. This applied to consumer products, but also to welfare products such as health and social care. The application of Fordism to welfare was particularly evident in the organization of the British welfare state in the late 1940s. However, just as the mass producer and consumer are now becoming fragmented and individualized, so standardized health and social care are no longer seen as acceptable. Under the Fordist system of production, standardization and consistency kept costs under control and defined what could be produced at an acceptable cost. The consumer's choices were limited by that fact. In the post-Fordist situation, with its fragmented production and consumption patterns and individualized consumer requirements, costs are more difficult to control, and it becomes necessary to ensure that each product separately constitutes value for money. Standardization is no longer available as a way of achieving that end. The quality of each product becomes an issue in itself and producers can no longer rely on a consensus that will persuade the consumer of the appropriateness of the product for them.

In the late 1940s the welfare state in the UK was created around large-scale providers of care, and it was those providers, rather than the consumers, who defined the acceptability of that care in terms of value for money. This situation was sustained by different features of the system in different sectors. In health care the power of the medical profession to define an acceptable level of health care was for many years unchallenged. The structure of the service itself made it difficult to challenge that power from within, and the social status of the medical profession made it equally difficult for the lay public to challenge from without. In the case of social care neither the service providers (local authorities) nor the occupational groups involved had anything like the advantages of the medical profession, but the low social status of many of their clients, and the stigma of receiving social care, had a similarly disempowering effect on the consumer.

On one level we can see that the general social and cultural change from a Fordist to a post-Fordist system explains the emergence of quality assurance. However, we need to build upon this with a look at specific processes in the history of health and social care over the past 40 years which provide a more complete explanation.

The proverbial visitor from Mars could reasonably expect quality assurance in health care and social care to have long histories – as long as the history of the provisions themselves – and consequently to have had many decades in which to develop sophisticated methods of measuring and assuring quality. If for no other reason, such a visitor might have this expectation because of the importance of health and social care to the general well-being, and in some cases the survival, of their recipients. At least in the case of health care the entire population is likely to have a stake at some point in optimizing the quality of care, and the imperative to do this would seem to be overwhelming. It is interesting, then, to discover that quality assurance as applied to health and social care is largely a phenomenon of the last twenty years, and that for many decades after the foundation of the British welfare state – not to mention the decades prior to that – quality assurance was a unknown concept. We must ask why.

Influences in health and social care

The evident features of health and social care which seem to dictate that they need to be provided as effectively as possible (and that this needs to be monitored and measured) disguise to some degree the underlying social dynamics of those two provisions, which until relatively recently have led in rather different directions.

In the case of health care we can locate the major dynamic in the historic dominance of medicine, and of the medical profession, which was generally inimical to the development of quality assurance as a distinctive concept. Higgs (1997) describes how medicine in the nineteenth century came to be dominated by hospitals, and by hospital-based consultants. The institutional tradition represented by the hospital system operated within a hierarchical structure in medicine that encouraged conservatism. The training of doctors was dominated by hospitals and consultants characterized by an adherence to established methods of treatment endorsed by dominant groups in the profession. This may seem a paradoxical point in the context of a period when medical progress was unprecedented. But this progress took place in the face of a significant degree of conservatism within medicine. Significantly, medicine was not often challenged from outside the profession in the first half of the twentieth century, and by the 1900s its power and prestige in the community as a whole was protection against such questioning. It seems then that what Maxwell (1984) calls the 'collective allergy' of the medical profession toward systematic external review can be explained historically. It is interesting that Ellis and Whittington (1993) identify the nursing profession rather than the medical profession as the most active of the health care professions in relation to developing quality assurance. Nursing has traditionally had a more open boundary to the outside world in terms of scrutiny of its practice than has medicine, and the creation of systems of quality monitoring involving persons from outside the profession on the whole presents less of a challenge to nurses than it does to doctors.

Different factors were at work in relation to social care. Whereas health care has an output which has been assumed (perhaps erroneously) to be understood and agreed in concrete terms by the lay population, the same cannot be said of social care. In particular this cannot be said of social work, whose output is generally perceived as problematic, within as well as outside the profession. This clearly creates problems for quality assurance of a different kind from those within health care. As Clarke (1993) recounts, the origins of social care lie in a moral enterprise to control and contain certain marginal elements in society. These activities were initiated on the whole because it was thought morally right, and a good investment for public order. But there was no criterion available for the early days of social care equivalent to the medical criterion of restoration to good health. It was only as the social sciences developed during the twentieth century that it became possible to start to think about social care in terms of outcomes. The identification of juvenile delinquency as a social ill, and the development of an explanatory model by Burt (1944), presented an early opportunity for the social care world (particularly the probation service) to work to more specific goals – the successful 'treatment' of young offenders.

Sapsford (1993) describes the development of indices of personal stability and adjustment in the middle decades of the century to reflect the developing models of social and psychological health in areas of psychiatry, clinical psychology and penology. These models were seen as variously applicable to individual behaviour, family dynamics and relationships, and community life. They were developed with particular frequency in the United States, in the context of the movement for community mental health (see for instance Caplan 1969), and provided a set of outcomes for social care which could be regarded as in some sense scientific. This latter status was perhaps further emphasized by the association with psychiatry and clinical psychology, which were perceived among those involved in social care as having a more developed scientific basis. The popularity of behaviourism (see for instance Jehu *et al.* 1972) and of family therapy among social workers at that time is an indication of the desire for validated and testable models for the evaluation of outcomes. The problem in the UK was that most social care was and is delivered in circumstances which make it very difficult to use such models of practice on a scale where outcomes can be evaluated in a systematic way. So the development of measurable therapies did little for quality assurance in social care.

The other agenda that sought to develop social care beyond its moral origins was the radical political agenda which again emerged during the 1960s and had a significant impact on the debate over social work's development in the 1970s. The writings of radical social work commentators were primarily focused on ideology and activism, and the notion that the results of social work input could be measured and evaluated in a consensual way were seen as unacceptable (see for instance Bailey and Brake 1980; Bolger *et al.* 1981). This stage of radical social work made little impact on actual practice, and even less on the organization of social care. But it did have an effect on its ideological underpinnings for many social workers, and may have contributed to an atmosphere of suspicion of measurable results in social care.

Quality assurance in health care

The development of the quality assurance agenda in health care can be traced to the 1970s after a number of issues had started to disturb the supposed consensus concerning the organization and functioning of the NHS during the 1950s and 1960s. First, a series of failures in health care were exposed which affected the confidence of the public in the health service and also had a considerable impact on planners, professionals and politicians. These included several scandals in the mental health sector in the late 1960s and early 1970s. The assumption made at the creation of the NHS that the professional competence of the medical profession was the best guarantee of an acceptable level of medical care began to be questioned. At the same time financial crises affecting the economics and public finances of western states forced the planners, politicians and professionals to consider how the increasing level of expenditure on health care might be controlled, and whether it would be possible to find ways of ensuring that that money was spent appropriately.

The arrival of the Thatcher government in 1979 gave a considerable fillip to the idea of 'value for money' and a greater commitment to the control of costs. Whereas the previous Labour government had had economies forced on it by economic and financial problems, the Thatcher government was, as Edgell and Duke (1991) point out, ideologically committed to the reduction of public expenditure as a goal in its own right. The introduction of general managers and of 'managerialism' into the NHS in the 1980s was intended by the government as a move toward more coherent planning and cost control. As Morris and Bell (1995) point out, this involved among other things the setting of targets and performance indicators, which provided steps toward quality measurement. Also, the need for managers to manage inevitably led them into conflict with the medical profession, and initiated a challenge to medical power which became a central feature of the health care system in ensuing years. Implicit in this challenge was a concern about the cost-effectiveness of medical care. However, medicine was not the only subject of managerial scrutiny. Nursing and other professions in health care were also having their practice subjected to similar questions, and the functioning of the service as a whole was under scrutiny. The reforms of the 1990 NHS and Community Care Act simply served to increase the pressure to achieve value for money by building that pressure into the system of the internal market. In addition, for the first time the 1990 Act included an explicit requirement for medical audit (DoH 1989a), which provided a powerful incentive for the development of more sophisticated methods of quality measurement.

However, the pressure to maximize quality was not simply a top-down pressure from government. Pressures were also starting to come from a number of other directions. As Ellis and Whittington (1993) recount, the medical profession itself was becoming increasingly aware during the 1960s and 1970s that their internal mechanisms for ensuring standards of practice needed to be more sophisticated, and a number of reports emerged from the medical profession expressing this concern. At the same time the practices of the medical profession were coming under increasing scrutiny from social scientists and economists, whose findings suggested that a good deal of what doctors do is unlikely to maximize their output as purveyors of good health. The development of health economics as a discipline has contributed greatly to the atmosphere of questioning and scepticism about the effectiveness of medicine in particular and health care in general (see for instance Mooney 1992). An increasing awareness that the health profile of the population would not necessarily be best improved by a traditional medical approach of treatment and cure showed itself, as Klein (1995) points out, even in statements of government policy such as *The Health of the Nation* (DoH 1992). Developments in medicine itself also propelled the same process forward, as the criteria for judging the success of particular treatments were developed and improved and the clinical trial, in particular, emerged as the template of medical research. Sackett *et al.* (1998) point out that medical treatments were often chosen through deduction on the basis of knowledge of pathophysiology and knowledge of the immediate physiological effects of particular treatments, without systematic study of the outcomes of such treatments. The development of evidence-based medicine, based on the systematic study of outcomes, can be seen as part of the same process of scrutiny.

Outside medicine it was becoming more widely understood that major health problems such as heart disease and cancer were not generally 'curable', and that prevention and control were more relevant goals. In the context of these problems it becomes difficult to know what constitutes effective medical care of those who are ill. It also raises a question as to how effective prevention might be measured. The development of health promotion as a preventive strategy helped also to promote an alternative model of health, described by Bunton and Burrows (1995) as 'late modern' in contrast to the 'modern' biomedical model. The nature of health was increasingly a matter of debate, and a positive view of health (for instance the World Health Organization (1946) definition as physical, mental and social well-being) was being set against the traditional biomedical view of health as the absence of disease. This shift in perception tended to pose new questions about the goals of health care and the criteria for judging its effectiveness. If successful health promotion meant improving the general well-being of the population, how might general well-being be measured? The problem here, as Bowling (1997) makes clear, is that it can be measured in numerous different ways, and that such measurements will not necessarily produce the same results. Arising out of these same processes of redefining health has been a changing public perception of risk and uncertainty in health. Environmental threats and the development of AIDS have created an awareness of global problems that cannot be easily controlled, and a sense of anxiety and frustration that the existing machinery of health care clearly cannot contain these of itself. This is linked by writers such as Nettleton (1995) to the increasing individualization of culture which has changed and to some extent removed some of the supports through which people coped with threats in the past. A desire to demonstrate measurable quality of output on the part of health providers as a way of restoring public faith is an understandable response to such anxieties.

Quality assurance in social care

In social care the development of quality assurance has followed a different route. Whereas the breakdown of traditional assumptions about what constituted good health care helped to promote the development of quality assurance in health care, the opposite happened in social care. The traditional lack of consensus about what constituted good social care, and in particular good social work, became intolerable to various groups for several reasons. In terms of public impatience with social workers' apparent uncertainty about what they should be doing, child protection has been a pivotal area in the 1970s and 1980s. A series of celebrated failures in child protection during this period led to an increasing public demand for systematic scrutiny of social workers' effectiveness. The mixture of reactive policing and prevention characteristic of this area created considerable difficulties of monitoring, but nonetheless it has been subjected to a kind of quality checking, in the form of a series of inquiries following major failures of child protection. However, as Harding (1997) points out, this particular method of quality checking has proved highly unsatisfactory, as these inquiries have generally been appointed reactively and unsystematically in response to media and public pressure; and effects on policy have been influenced by the ideological agendas of various interest groups. Because of difficulties in establishing probability, cause and effect in this area, the main focus of monitoring has inevitably been on procedures and processes rather than on outcomes.

In the 1980s the movement in social work and social services toward anti-discriminatory practice (see for instance Phillipson 1988) provided another boost for the idea that social care can formulate clear goals and evaluate itself by reference to these. This development, although essentially a moral and political exercise, differed from the radicalism of the 1970s in that it has expressed itself in a commitment to the achievement of measurable practical outcomes. The close and earnest self-examination in terms of practice and theory that this development encouraged at individual, group and organizational level contributed significantly to a culture of quality assurance in social care.

Other factors also contributed to the change of culture and practice. The squeezing of local government finances in the 1980s produced a greater concern for cost-effectiveness, and the NHS and Community Care Act sought to encourage the more effective use of resources in community care, by developing needs-led rather than service-led provision (DoH 1989b). The Act focused on quality in social care in two ways. First, the change of role of local authority from provider to commissioner required local authorities to consider the quality of the care they were commissioning from other agencies. Second, the Act introduced a specific requirement for local authorities to set up separate inspection units to scrutinize services provided within their remit. These demands required those involved in social care to focus on ways of systematically measuring quality in social care, and this led to a good deal of focused consideration, exemplified in works such as Kelly and Warr (1992) which explored a number of dimensions in social care quality assurance. A further fillip for quality assurance has come from the post-1997 Labour government, which has sought to encourage a more clearly results-oriented approach to social care, embodied in the concept of Best Value (DoH 1998).

Problems and issues

I have suggested that loss of perceived consensus has propelled health care toward quality assurance, while a perceived desire for a consensus where none existed has played the same role in relation to social care. However, it is not clear that quality assurance has the potential to create a new consensus about quality in either area. The fundamental question – what constitutes quality? – is not something that any quality assurance system can resolve, because that question has to be answered before a choice can be made as to which quality assurance system is used. Each system is based on certain propositions concerning the nature of quality, and to choose that system requires the user to 'buy into' those propositions. Such a choice must finally be made on the basis of ideology. In addition, quality assurance is beset by epistemological problems concerning the correct interpretation of evidence. This problem was recognized by Donabedian (1980) who accordingly included structure and process as well as outcome in his system of quality assurance, on the basis that outcomes do not always reflect the quality of input of treatment and care, given that health is affected by a multiplicity of factors. Where outcomes are not a reliable guide, a causal link between structures and processes on one hand, and outcomes on the other, can justify the assessment of structure and process.

In addition there are areas where issues of epistemology and issues of ideology overlap to produce problems of quality measurement. The measurement of general health state and quality of life both fall into this category. There are numerous alternative ways of measuring these phenomena as Farquahar (1995) points out, and as they would seem to be important outcomes, it is arguably important to be able to measure them consistently. The problem with this is in part an epistemological one of converting something which is partly subjective into a consistent quantifiable measurement. However, the other problem is that the factors that are included in these measurements are themselves matters of judgement. For instance, how far should quality of life emphasize freedom from pain, as against the achievement of goals? The balance is itself subjective and will differ in the context of differing ideologies.

On the matter of consensus on the definition of quality, Alazewski and Manthorpe (1993) suggest that this problem has been managed in a number of ways in different approaches to quality assurance. At one end of a possible continuum is what they term a universalist approach, operating generally on a system of external inspection. The assumption behind this approach is that it is possible to formulate and apply standards of quality which are not simply internal to a particular organization, but are universal to a system of care. An example of this might be the use of the 'Health of the Nation' outcomes as a quality template as advocated by Shaw (1997). At the other end of the spectrum is a pluralist approach, exemplified often in the work of quality circles, which does not depend on any pre-established definition of quality, but emphasizes rather a set of processes. Between these extremes are approaches which place the definition of quality with a particular protagonist in the process – for instance consumer, profession or organization.

All these approaches have different implications for the power balance in health and social care. The dominant system of the early 1990s, the internal market, offered the promise of empowering the consumer, but where the consumer is not a customer, and lacks the true leverage of the market, this does not happen. What *has* worked to some degree is that in the internal market system some of the real customers – the purchasers – have gained in terms of power, and the drive to quality assurance has been partly geared to meeting *their* requirements. This is true of health authorities to some degree, but is particularly true of fundholding GPs who in some cases, according to Glennerster (1998), have significantly influenced providers' approach to quality. However, none of this empowered the real consumer, the patient. The other approaches identified by Alazewski and Manthorpe (1993) locate power variously with the state, the professionals and the managers.

Impact of quality assurance

Quality assurance has the potential to perform two functions that have fundamentally different implications for health and social care. One function is that of constraint, in particular constraint on the freedom of providers of health and social care to decide for themselves what is an acceptable level of service. This is a constraint generally exercised through leverage by other bodies. The other function is facilitation, whereby providers are enabled to define and pursue their goals. These two functions can be seen as ends of a spectrum, and that spectrum can be applied to at least two levels, one relating to activity within organizations, and the other to transactions between organizations.

Within organizations

In terms of what happens within organizations, it can be argued that quality assurance has been used by government as a means of controlling the activities of providers of care. It has been used to replace the bonds of consensus and (in the case of health care) deference that held the health and social care systems together at the founding of the welfare state. The hierarchical relationship that determined interactions between doctors, other health care workers, patients and the general public enabled a workable degree of control to such an extent that governments were able to assume for many years that the NHS was cohesive and effective. When those assumptions were no longer tenable, specific mechanisms were necessary to exert control over the health care system. The 1979 Conservative government introduced a number of such mechanisms, all of which sought to mobilize the NHS into the government's agenda, while at the same time minimizing the government's day-to-day responsibility for NHS activities. The encouragement of quality assurance fitted well into this strategy. Working in tandem with the internal market, it allowed government to impose an agenda on health providers while denying responsibility for the way that agenda was pursued. In that context quality is that which adheres to standards expressing the central policy agenda. Prior (1989) argues that quality assurance in social care represents an agenda of control of the activities of care providers through commodification and reduction of those activities to measurable behavioural units, divorced from the reality of human experience. Herein lies the constraint. If the definition of quality imposed on the organization restricts quality assurance to those aspects of its output which are quantifiable, this will inevitably constrain the activity of the organization by restricting its priorities to the more mechanistic aspects of its output. The context of Prior's discussion is the fundamental problem of reducing any complex human experience to measurable units. In this respect most quality assurance simplifies, but whether that simplification is essentially reductive depends in part on whether any serious attempt is made to evaluate the unquantifiable human aspects of care. Such an exercise is bound to be imperfect but it has the virtue of ensuring that the human aspects of care remain in the quality frame, however roughly, in a systematic attempt to evaluate quality. The problem arises, as Prior suggests, where caring activities are reduced to measurable units for the purpose of controlling costs, and only the most easily costed parts of the process are included in the definition of quality. Market pressures will tend to increase the likelihood that this will happen.

At the other end of the spectrum, quality assurance can facilitate creativity and innovation. This requires a shared concept of quality to become a value within the culture of an organization, and for the consistent pursuit of that quality to become a norm in that culture. For this to happen, the underpinning principles of quality assurance need to be owned by those working in the organization, and need to come to be seen as part of their repertoire. A culture of quality assurance, like any living culture, is bound to evolve over time, and by virtue of that fact quality assurance could no longer be simply an instrument of external control. However, organizations in health and social care include highly diverse workforces, and such a culture can only become a reality if it unites different groups. As Maxwell (1984) points out, the medical profession has always been resistant to having its practice scrutinized by outsiders but Dent (1995) describes how the medical profession has moved slowly (though not completely) toward a willingness to engage in quality assurance procedures over the past 30 years. However, this is not a simple or a complete process and Klein (1998) suggests that the bringing together of organizational and professional approaches to quality remains a major problem. The account by Ferlie *et al.* (1999) of the behaviour of a group of orthopaedic surgeons in relation to quality assurance suggests that this group at least does not share a common culture of quality assurance with the wider system, despite a group-specific commitment to quality. Part of the problem may be that Alazewski and Manthorpe's (1993) alternative models do not mix, or at least have not successfully been mixed as yet. Such quality procedures as continual quality improvement and total quality management seem most likely to have a real impact on the culture of the organization, but they remain essentially organizational procedures, more likely to commend themselves to managers than to the professionals. Goldmann's (1997) account of the use of CQI in an Israeli hospital suggests that this feature may actively alienate the professionals.

At worst, mechanisms of quality assurance can be a substitute for a norm of quality assurance, in that they require the personnel involved to engage in quality assurance activities, which they are not inclined to do. However, that could not be sustained in the longer run. To bring about long-term change such mechanisms must also bring about cultural change so that quality assurance comes to be seen as having a normal and legitimate claim on time and energy. An important requirement for this to happen is that the procedures enable personnel to engage in a real way with the idea of quality, even if its definition is seen as problematic in a given situation. Procedures which fail in this are not likely to have a positive effect on culture. Again, the experience of using CQI reported by Goldmann illustrates this. Pollitt (1996) argues that some business-oriented methods have much to offer health care, but suggests also that they can only succeed if applied within very precise parameters. However, the most recent approach to the problem of creating an inclusive culture of quality assurance may have more to offer. Clinical governance, introduced by the Labour government in 1999, seeks to recruit the professionals into the quality agenda by placing them at the centre of it, and attempting to create a seamless continuum of organizational and professional responsibility. Buetow and Roland (1999) suggest that clinical governance may overcome some of the problems that have bedevilled other approaches, but in order to do this it must provide sufficient incentives for the professionals to accept a closer involvement with organizational priorities.

Between organizations

In terms of what happens between organizations, we can again see a spectrum of transactions between the constraining and the facilitative. It is clear that quality assurance can be seen as a component of the market mechanism. It functions alongside price as a definer of value for money. In particular, it acts as a countervailing factor against the tendency for quality to be squeezed in order to minimize price. One of the concerns widely expressed in relation to the introduction of the internal market in health and community care in the early 1990s was that the pressure to keep costs down would compromise the quality of care. Quality assurance can act as a counterbalance to this. However, it is as difficult for a commissioning body to decide what quality it wants as it is for a provider to decide what quality it can achieve. In this situation the very fact of having quality assurance procedures becomes a substitute for the ability to deliver demonstrable quality. Being committed to quality is rather like being against sin. It is, as Klein (1998) points out, 'a hurrah word, capable of many interpretations, to which everyone can subscribe' (p. 51). It could be argued that far from being constraining this situation is freeing in that it allows providers to get away with a show of quality without the substance. However, the market relationship includes constraints even in this situation. Quality assurance as a means to market survival belongs within the framework of relationships which Hunter (1997) argued were typical of the market reforms of 1990 – characterized by competition, mistrust, conflicting goals and partial, strategic communication. Each organization in the market is constrained by the demands and disciplines of the market to ensure that its definition of quality, and its mechanisms for assuring it, are acceptable to customers. In that sense it has an essentially constraining effect on the dealings between organizations in the market arena, and on the development of quality as an intrinsic characteristic of their output.

However, it is possible for quality assurance to be facilitative in relation to transactions between organizations. It is clear that the relationship between organizations involved in delivering health and social care can be characterized in a number of different ways. Market-style competition was imposed by the Conservative government in 1990, and has to a degree been removed by the Labour government in 1999. Other kinds of non-market competition may still persist – for instance competition for resources – in a way that they have always existed. But some relationships require cooperation rather than competition between organizations. Some organizations commission the work of others, and are in a relationship of accountability based on contract. Some organizations are in a stakeholder relationship to others, involving arguable (though ill-defined) moral obligations. The 1999 Health Act places an obligation on organizations in health care to cooperate with one another. They are also in a relationship to those bodies which confer legitimacy on their existence and their operation, and to whom they are accountable. For most component organizations in the NHS the legitimizing body is central government, while for local government agencies it is a combination of central government and the local electorate. Care-giving bodies also have a relationship with the recipients of their services, which is not one of accountability but is nonetheless one of obligation. All of these bodies have expectations of the care provided by provider organizations, and to some degree these expectations are based on agreement with the provider, constituting an implicit or explicit contract. Quality assurance can be seen as an expression of the obligation expressed in that contract, and quality in that context is synonymous with that which is contracted for.

Conclusion

It may be that the post-market situation will allow a more facilitative version of quality assurance to develop in the context of these relationships. The removal of market relationships does not remove pressure to keep costs down, and the temptation to judge quality by what is measurable in resource use will not disappear. However, it may be that it will be possible in the longer term to establish a different relationship between organizations in health and social care, based on trust – the sort of relationship that Hunter identified as operating within the NHS before the 1990 changes. And that change, if it occurs, will offer an opportunity for a significant change in the function of quality assurance. The fact that quality as a concept is multifaceted and problematic is something that cannot be acknowledged in the context of market relationships. But it can be allowed to enter the equation where a sufficient level of trust exists between those engaged in the transaction. This allows greater freedom to negotiate an agreed definition of quality that may deviate from established definitions and thereby allow innovation and creativity. This would allow both commissioner and provider organizations to be more creative in their response to the needs of consumers. However, to achieve this, two requirements would have to be met. First, each of the organizations involved would need to foster an internal culture of creative quality assurance, to generate the innovations that would be currency between organizations. And second, the state would need to ensure that a firm structure of interorganizational obligations was kept in place. The Labour government has tried to replace a culture of competition with a culture of cooperation. But the motivation to cooperate needs to be sustained by a clear model of interorganizational obligations which are taken on board as moral norms as well as regulatory requirements. The ethics of organizational behaviour and interorganizational relationships have developed as a discipline to a point where a conceptual framework for characterizing these relationships is a possibility (see for instance Spencer *et al.* 2000) and could be applied to a duty-based view of quality assurance. However, such a framework needs to be formalized in the structural relationships of organizations in health and social care, and this can only be achieved by government.

References

Alazewski, A. and Manthorpe, J. (1993) Quality and the welfare services: a literature review, *British Journal of Social Work*, 23: 653–65.

Bailey, M. and Brake, M. (1980) *Radical Social Work and Practice*. London: Edward Arnold.

Bolger, S., Corrigan, P., Docking, J. and Frost, N. (1981) *Toward Socialist Welfare Work: Working in the State*. London: Macmillan.

Bowling, A. (1997) *Measuring Health: A Review of Quality of Life Measurement Scales*, 2nd edn. Buckingham: Open University Press.

Buetow, S. and Roland, M. (1999) Clinical governance: bridging the gap between managerial and clinical approaches to quality of care, *Quality in Health Care*, 8: 184–90.

Bunton, R. and Burrows, R. (1995) Consumption and health in the epidemiological clinic of late modern medicine, in R. Bunton, S. Nettleton and R. Burrows (eds) *The Sociology of Health Promotion*. London: Routledge.

Burt, C. (1944) *The Young Delinquent*, 4th edn. Bickley: London University Press.

Caplan, G. (1969) *An Approach to Community Mental Health*. London: Tavistock.

Clarke, J. (1993) The comfort of strangers: social work in context, in J. Clarke (ed.) *A Crisis in Care? Challenges to Social Work*. London: Sage Publications.

Dent, M. (1995) Doctors, peer review and quality assurance, in T. Johnson, G. Larkin and M. Saks (eds) *Health Professions and the State in Europe*. London: Routledge.

DoH (Department of Health) (1989a) *Working for Patients*. London: HMSO.

DoH (Department of Health) (1989b) *Caring for People: Community Care in the Next Decade and Beyond*. London: HMSO.

DoH (Department of Health) (1992) *The Health of the Nation: A Strategy for Health in England*. London: HMSO.

DoH (Department of Health) (1998) *Modernising Social Services: Promoting Independence, Improving Protection, Raising Standards*. London: HMSO.

Dominelli, L. (1988) *Anti-Racist Social Work*. Basingstoke: Macmillan.

Donabedian, A. (1980) *Explorations in Quality Assessment and Monitoring, Vol. 1: The Definition of Quality and Approaches to its Assessment*. Ann Arbor, MI: Health Administration Press.

Edgell, S. and Duke, V. (1991) *A Measure of Thatcherism*. London: HarperCollins.

Ellis, R. and Whittington, D. (1993) *Quality Assurance in Health Care: A Handbook*. London: Edward Arnold.

Farquahar, M. (1995) Definitions of quality of life: a taxonomy, *Journal of Advanced Nursing*, 22: 502–7.

Ferlie, E., Wood, M. and Fitzgerald, L. (1999) Some limits to evidence-based medicine: a case study from elective orthopaedics, *Quality in Health Care*, 8: 99–107.

Glennerster, H. (1998) Competition and quality in health care: the UK experience, *International Journal for Quality in Health Care*, 10: 403–10.

Goldmann, D. (1997) Sustaining CQI, *International Journal for Quality in Health Care*, 9: 7–9.

Harding, L. F. (1997) *Perspectives in Child Care Policy*, 2nd edn. London: Longman.

Higgs, P. (1997) The limits of medical knowledge, in G. Scambler (ed.) *Sociology as Applied to Medicine*, 4th edn. London: Saunders.

Hunter, D. (1997) *Desperately Seeking Solutions*. London: Addison-Wesley-Longman.

Jehu, D., Hardiker, P., Yelloly, M. and Shaw, M. (1972) *Behaviour Modification in Social Work*. London: Wiley.

Kelly, D. and Warr, B. (1992) *Quality Counts: Achieving Quality in the Social Care Services*. London: Whiting and Birch.

Klein, R. (1995) *The New Politics of the National Health Service*, 3rd edn. London: Longman.

Klein, R. (1998) Can policy drive quality? *Quality in Health Care* 7 (Supplement): 51–3.

Maxwell, R. J. (1984) Quality assessment in health, *British Medical Journal*, 228: 1470–7.

Mooney, G. (1992) *Economics, Medicine and Health Care*. London: Harvester.

Morris, B. and Bell, L. (1995) Quality in health care, in J. Glynn and D. Perkins, *Managing Health Care: Challenges for the 90s*. London: Saunders.

Navarro, V. (1994) *The Politics of Health Policy*. Cambridge, MA: Blackwell.

Nettleton, S. (1995) *The Sociology of Health and Illness*. Cambridge: Polity.

Pollitt, C. (1996) Business approaches to quality improvement: why they are hard for the NHS to swallow, *Quality in Health Care*, 5: 104–10.

Prior, L. (1989) Evaluation research and quality assurance, in J. Gubrium and D. Silverman, *The Politics of Field Research*. London: Sage Publications.

Sackett, D., Richardson, W. S., Rosenberg, W. and Haynes, R. B. (1998) *Evidence-Based Medicine: How to Teach and Practise EBM*. London: Churchill Livingstone.

Sapsford, R. (1993) Understanding people: the growth of an expertise, in J. Clarke (ed.) *A Crisis in Care? Challenges to Social Work*. London: Sage Publications.

Shaw, I. (1997) Assessing quality in mental health care: the United Kingdom experience, *Evaluation Review*, 21: 364–70.

Spencer, E., Mills, A., Rorty, M. and Werhane, P. (2000) *Organization Ethics in Health Care*. New York, NY: Oxford University Press.

World Health Organization (1946) *Constitution*. Geneva: WHO.

chapter nine

PRIORITIZING AND RATIONING

Introduction

Prioritizing and rationing are not in any logical sense opposites, and they are often discussed in the health care context as being similar, equivalent or even identical. Certainly the two terms have come to be applied to solutions to the same problem. The problem concerned is the discrepancy between available resources and the possible uses of those resources, whether those uses are identified by reference to need or demand or to some other criterion. Generally more uses can be justified for health and social care resources than there are resources to be used, and the problem is one of resource allocation. Who gets what, and who does without what?

Definitions

Rationing can be defined as the allocation of scarce resources in such a way that they are withheld from some of those who could benefit from those resources. These decisions are often (though not always) taken at the individual level. Prioritizing is generally understood to involve decisions about who gets first claim on resources. These decisions tend to be taken on a 'macro' rather than a 'micro' scale (Klein *et al.* 1996). By that definition they seem to represent two aspects or stages of the same process, with prioritizing as the 'macro' stage emphasizing provision, and rationing as the 'micro' stage emphasizing withholding. Writers such as Hunter (1997) treat the two concepts as not importantly different.

However, Klein *et al.* (1996) see them as different processes, although aimed at the same outcome. If we look at the debate on resource allocation in health and social care in recent years, it is clear that there is a real difference in connotation, with rationing carrying a negative image and prioritizing being seen more positively. This is not surprising. Rationing does not only emphasize withholding. It also involves withholding from identifiable individuals whose names, faces and lives (and deaths) often make good media stories (see for instance Richardson and Waddington's (1996) discussion of the Jaymee Bowen case). Prioritizing is more impersonal. In political terms acknowledgement of rationing has been assiduously avoided by government (Smith 1993) until recently, probably for this reason, whereas the notion of prioritizing is an acceptable part of political discourse. So we might suspect that these are different ways – 'nice' and 'nasty' ways – of dressing up the same basic activity.

However, the two terms have come to be associated with rather different ways of approaching the problem of limited resources in health care. Prioritizing has come to be associated with a process of deciding what kind of treatments will be made available within a health care system and what kinds will not. There is an identifiable trend for that process to be undertaken in a way that is open and consultative to varying degrees, and at various levels. Notable examples of this process are the public health care systems of Oregon (Kitzhaber 1993) and the Netherlands (Government Committee on Choices in Health Care 1992). In both these cases the state's political leadership and health bureaucracies undertook an exercise of consultative prioritizing, leading to the compiling of a list of those treatments that would be available within the state's health care system. Treatments omitted from the list would have to be bought by the individual patient. In the case of Oregon the process of selecting treatments to be included involved a protracted and elaborate process of public consultation, involving town meetings, phone polls and focus groups. Lightfoot (1995) argues that there is also a policy aspiration toward the obtaining of user views in the case of social care prioritizing and that this is perhaps more likely to be achieved in social than in health care because of the fact that social care is less dominated than health care by the idea of professional expertise, represented in particular by the medical profession.

Rationing by contrast tends to be associated with individual decisions about individual withholding of a particular treatment from a particular person. So the focus is on who gets a liver transplant and who does not, and who gets Viagra and who does not, rather than on the money that is spent overall on liver transplants as against money spent on Viagra. However, this is not the whole story. Rationing can be divided into two rather different processes. One kind of rationing involves the making of conscious individual choices as to who will receive a treatment and who will not. These fall into Klein *et al.*'s (1996) categories of rationing by selection and denial. The other kind is what we might term 'systemic' rationing, where treatments are rationed, not through a conscious decision by any particular person that a given individual should not have it, but rather as a result of the working of a system which in effect conserves resources. The best example of this kind of mechanism is the waiting list, which withholds over a period of time; but there are other methods. Hunter (1997), among others, identifies rationing by deterrence and dilution, and we can see these as essentially systemic. Making a service so unattractive that it will not be sought except by the desperate, or so meagre that there is enough for everyone, need involve no individual decisions. Despite their differences, systemic rationing and individual rationing share an opposite tendency from that of prioritizing – a tendency to be protected from outside scrutiny. Individual decisions to withhold treatment are very often made by individual clinicians and as such are not public and not easily accessible to outside scrutiny. The reasons for making such a decision are also not easily scrutinized as they are often seen as matters of clinical judgement. Rationing by deterrence or dilution are likely to be politically uncomfortable and therefore relatively covert.

Rationing and prioritizing in context

The operation of rationing and prioritizing in health and social care in the UK is characterized by a slow and as yet incomplete acknowledgement of the reality of these processes by government and public opinion. In Hunter's account, prioritizing seems to have happened very little as a conscious process in the first three decades of the existence of the NHS (Hunter 1997). After 1974 machinery was put in place to enable rational planning, and therefore prioritizing, at national and local levels (Ham 1999) but Small (1990) argues that the economic problems that followed in the mid- to late 1970s meant that prioritizing took a rather different form from that intended, emerging not as a positive directional planning process but as a way of coping with diminishing resources. Inevitably prioritizing decisions at national and local levels were partly processes of political power broking, with parts of the medical profession exerting a good deal of influence. Some sectors prospered, other sectors did not. For instance, mental health services consistently did badly during this period. One positive development in the midst of the problems of the late 1970s was the creation of the Resource Allocation Working Party to rectify inequalities in health care provision between regions of Britain. Although the priority given to underresourced regions was modest, the cumulative effect of this over years was significant in reducing inequities in health provision (Whitehead 1994). However, Gray and

Jenkins (1995) describe how planning activities generally became decentralized after the 1990 reforms. Despite a slow beginning, health authorities increasingly took on a rationing role, as reported by Court (1995), with measures such as excluding particular treatments from the list of those they would finance. These included some forms of fertility treatment (Redmayne and Klein 1993). Localization clearly had drawbacks in relation to consistency and accountability, and one of the legacies of this process is the problem of 'postcode rationing' whereby provision varies by district. However, a positive outcome during subsequent years was that some health authorities put a significant amount of energy and ingenuity into involving their populations in the prioritizing process (see for example Hope et al. 1998).

Individual rationing in health care has traditionally been within the power of the medical profession who have, however, been deeply ambivalent about the exercise of that function. Hope et al. (1993) argue that the term 'not clinically indicated' is often used in a highly ambiguous way by doctors, and may mean either 'not in the patient's interests' or 'not the right use of resources'. The latter use can disguise a rationing decision, and there is evidence of rationing decisions being presented in clinical terms, as a decision to withhold a given treatment because that treatment would not be helpful to the patient. This has been identified in a number of areas. Baker (1993) reports a similar process with regard to renal transplants where an age-based rationing policy was conducted by consultants, ostensibly on clinical grounds but in effect treating age as a rationing criterion. So on one hand there are true clinical considerations which might lead a doctor to withhold a particular treatment even where that treatment is abundantly available; considerations such as the futility, harmfulness or marginal benefits of a treatment. On the other hand there are true rationing issues, only relevant where treatment is in short supply, as in the situation where a patient stands to benefit significantly from a treatment, but less than another patient, and there is not enough to go round.

In the first few decades of the life of the NHS the position of the medical profession allowed this process to be accepted by patients, who often passively accepted that a life-saving treatment would not be available to them because they could not benefit from it, whereas in fact the treatment would have benefited them but the doctor thought it was an inappropriate use of limited resources. This situation has changed over the last two decades, as the problems of resourcing the health service have become a more explicit part of public debate, and the need to ration and prioritize has become impossible to conceal, despite being publicly ignored by governments. The reforms of 1990 created an internal market which exposed resource problems and exposed also the need to ration, as purchasers (health authorities and fundholding GPs) decided what services they could afford to purchase for their population and what services they would have to forgo. According to Smith and Morissey (1994) and Toon (1994), fundholding GPs, faced with the task of making a finite fund cover a given patient population over a given period, were placed under pressure to ration on an individual basis also. This has been accompanied by a cultural change in the doctor–patient relationship, making passive patient acceptance of rationing decisions less likely. Patients have become less willing to believe that the doctor knows best, and more questioning and demanding.

These competing pressures – on the one hand to ration and prioritize, and on the other to be held accountable for rationing and prioritizing decisions – have been accompanied by the development of rational models of rationing and prioritizing to assist decision makers in these activities. These models generally rely on the principle of utility – maximizing health gain – to distinguish between treatments and between patients, and in this sense show the stamp of the growing discipline of health economics which started to influence the thinking of planners, professionals and politicians during the 1980s. The best-known model is probably quality adjusted life years (QALYs) (Williams 1985), developed in the influential health economics unit at York University, which works on the principle that decisions about the use of health care resources would be determined by the ability of a particular treatment to increase the quality of life of a given patient over a given period of time. Although QALYs has been presented as a means of choosing between treatments, its critics, such as Harris (1991), have argued that it is also, and more importantly, an instrument for choosing between patients.

Despite all this, government has through much of the period since 1990 avoided acknowledging responsibility for rationing decisions, and to some degree denied the need to ration, though the need to prioritize *is* acknowledged (Smith 1993). The decentralization of the NHS effected by the 1990 reforms provided a suitable structure for shifting rationing responsibility down to purchasers, and that shift was exploited by government until nearly the end of the 1990s. However, pressure for an open public debate on rationing, promoted in particular by the King's Fund (New 1997), seems to have had some impact on the terms of discussion. Ferriman (1999) reports that in 1999 the Secretary of State took what appears to be a rationing decision. He decided that the drug Viagra would be made available to some categories of patients and not others. This seems to be part of a shift in government thinking toward an acknowledgement of rationing, built into the machinery of the 1999 NHS reforms. Under those reforms health authorities continue to prioritize. GPs are no longer required to ration on an individual basis but have ceded this role to the primary care groups/trusts which, as Pickard and Sheaff (1999) note, have a major rationing role.

In social care there is a history of awareness that resources are often insufficient to meet need as perceived by clients, and that some resources will therefore be withheld from individuals who could benefit from them. These issues were discussed by Judge twenty years ago (Judge 1978). Rationing by waiting list has certainly featured in social care, but services for clients in greater difficulty have generally been allocated on the basis of individual decisions, which has meant withholding the service from some clients, and providing it for others. Before 1990 there is evidence of a good deal of individual discretion being exercised by social workers. Local variations in resourcing and the subjective nature of some of the judgements needed in deciding who will and who will not receive a particular resource meant that the rationing role for social workers could not be, and was not, denied. After the implementation of the 1990 NHS and Community Care Act discretion in rationing diminished according to Ellis *et al.* (1999), while the need to ration remained. In fact the process of care purchasing and care management has allowed rationing to become somewhat more formalized, as more explicit decisions can be made about cost as a focus for organized negotiation between professionals and managers within localities; though, as Leat and Perkins (1998) point out, this in itself needs a good deal of creativity to make it work. In the context of both social care and health care it is probably fair to say that in general rationing is more individual and less consultative than prioritizing, and that it is dominated by the professionals and managers rather than by the politicians or the public; and also that it contrasts with the more public kinds of prioritizing in all these respects.

Distributive justice

Rationing and prioritizing are both characterized by conflict of interests, and the rationing and prioritizing decisions that are made reflect the interplay of interest groups and principles, fuelled by the exercise of power and the interchange of argument. Much centres round how to prioritize and how to ration. The paradigm of distributive justice has been argued by a number of writers to provide an ethical underpinning for social policy, both generally (Rawls 1971; Miller 1976) and in relation to rationing and prioritizing decisions (Daniels 1985). Distributive justice is not a unitary concept, however, but a composite of several principles in balance. Arguably the most fundamental of these is that of equality. Aristotle's definition of justice was the equal treatment of those who are equal in relevant respects. This is a somewhat 'thin' version of justice as it leaves open the question of what respects *are* relevant. But it can be 'thickened' by the Kantian notion of the moral specialness of the person (Paton 1978). All reasoning beings in Kant's philosophy are ends in themselves and have an irreducible moral importance which is, essentially, the same for each person. To treat one person as more important than another in fundamental ways (such as the maintenance of health) is to deny that common humanity. The other principles that we might use to achieve a just distribution of health and social care need to be weighed against the requirements of equality.

If equality provides a skeleton for distributive justice, the organs are provided by a set of principles which to some degree complement one another, and to some degree compete. These are generally agreed to include need, rights, desert and utility. I shall consider these in turn. In common-sense terms need is most widely recognized as a fair basis on which to prioritize or to ration, but as a concept need is problematic. In health care need for a treatment is widely defined (for instance by Hurley *et al.* 1997) as ability to benefit from that treatment or provision. However, need is also associated with the severity of the problem which the patient suffers. The first definition overlaps somewhat with utility, in that ability to benefit must relate closely to the prospect of help given being effective. And it would tend to exclude those whose situation is more severe and less tractable and whose need (in the other sense) is greatest. This gives an indication of the pervasive influence of the utility principle in health care in that it subsumes need to some degree. However, in social care, needs are seen more explicitly as the main basis for prioritizing and rationing, in the context of the post-1990 needs-led service. But the nature of need is even less clear in social care than in health care. Writers such as Miller (1976) and Doyal and Gough (1991) have attempted to identify fundamental needs, but there is no evidence of consensus on this, and Blackman argues that 'In public policy terms needs are essentially what the state decides to recognise and provide resources to meet' (Blackman 1998: 186).

There is also an issue of layers and levels of need. We might argue that a poor person who cannot afford a pair of shoes needs shoes. Or we could say that they need education, upskilling and support to become viable in the labour market, and cease to be poor. In a sense both needs exist, though the meeting of the deeper need will obviate the more surface need. There is no obviously fair way of deciding which need ought to be met by the providers of health or social care which focuses on need alone. Other factors then must come into the equation. Utility may provide a guide as to which need should be met. Deeper needs may be so difficult and expensive to meet as to be not worth attempting. As an example of this, Foster (1996) argues that, in the absence of evidence that health promotion is cost-effective in reducing health inequalities, the NHS should aim instead to ensure equal access to the treatments necessitated by those inequalities. On the other hand meeting surface needs – the classic 'sticking plaster' approach – may be far more wasteful of resources. Other factors, such as the obligations of the agency and the entitlements of the client, must also come into this. We have an interesting situation where the criterion of justice which probably has the highest cultural currency – need – seems to present some of the most difficult problems in application.

The relationship between entitlement and obligation – usually the entitlement of the client and the obligation of the agency or the state – provides the second major criterion of distributive justice. Often this relationship is referred to simply as rights. If it makes sense to say that the client has a right to a particular service, then it is just that they receive that service. But what gives the client a right to a service? Rights are often divided into two sorts, ideal or moral rights, and positive rights (Miller 1976). Ideal rights are claimed on the basis of general moral principles or characteristics which stand independently of any particular arrangements that provide those rights. For instance, the United Nations Charter of Human Rights is based on a belief that the fact of being human confers certain rights, and these rights are fundamental, existing prior to laws or other arrangements provided by human societies to provide those things that humans have a right to. These rights can be flouted, ignored by governments, and still be said to exist. Positive rights, by contrast, depend for their existence on practical arrangements providing for them. A right to unemployment benefit, for instance, only exists in the UK because legislation ordains that people in certain circumstances are entitled to unemployment benefit. Such rights are generally dependent on eligibility, and this is defined by the rules under which the service is made available.

In the context of prioritizing and rationing in social and health care, rights present some problems. Most of these provisions are somewhat different from such provisions as unemployment benefit, in that they are dependent on assessment by a professional gatekeeper. While the NHS and Community Care Act can be read as recognizing a positive right by the client to initial access to the gatekeeper, beyond that the concept of rights becomes attenuated by the gatekeeper's power to decide, generally on the basis of need and utility, what the client will get. It is difficult for the client to contest such decisions, and the client's right to any specific provision is therefore very much in doubt. As far as ideal rights are concerned, lack of a concrete reference point of justification makes such rights hard to argue, though in political terms they sometimes provide a basis for claims. For instance, arguments that older patients ought to have access to such treatments as liver transplants, even though the life years gained will be limited, can be sustained on the basis that their right to treatment is not diminished by age. This would have to be argued as an ideal right rather than a positive right, and a basis for that right would have to be found. One argument, that we have a right to that which we have been promised, might be used here on the basis of the undertakings made when the NHS was set up. However, it is a difficult argument. At the time of writing it is hard to say what impact the Human Rights Act (1998) will have on this situation. Most of the rights embodied therein can be seen as rights to particular liberties rather than as rights to be provided with specific goods. However, it may be that the right to life embodied in this legislation will be used to argue for the provision of life-saving treatment. If such arguments are accepted by the courts, the implications for resource allocation in this area will be considerable, and may well require existing practices to be radically revised.

The third principle that is sometimes used in the context of distributive justice is desert. The question is, does the patient or client *deserve* the service? On the whole this criterion is not one that is acceptable among those engaged in the provision of health and social care. Where it is observed to influence decisions it is seen as problematic, as by Ellis *et al.* (1999). However, it has some currency among the public in certain specific areas. Where patients have created their own disease through irresponsible behaviour, it could be argued that they deserve the treatment less than those who have developed the same illness by simple misfortune. Ways of becoming infected by the HIV virus are sometimes referred to in the media in a way that distinguishes the 'innocent', who were infected through blood transfusions, from those who were infected through sexual contact. There is some evidence that members of the public will give weight to whether or not a patient's liver failure is a result of alcohol consumption, for instance in the study by Neuberger *et al.* (1998). However, in general it seems to make little sense to prioritize or (more probably) ration in accordance with desert. This would seem to be using health and social care as a reward for good behaviour, and its withholding as a punishment. Institutionalized reward and punishment are arguably quite legitimate features of the social order, but health and social care seem unsuited to be used in this way.

The final component principle of distributive justice is that of maximizing well-being – of utility. This has been a goal of health and social policy in the UK since the days of John Stuart Mill (1962), whose philosophy of utilitarianism provides the intellectual basis for this aspiration. The simple principle is that actions should be judged by the degree to which they maximize an agreed good. Mill spoke in terms of maximizing happiness, but a health and social care system might sensibly seek another good such as health or well-being gained. This is less obviously a basic component of justice, though it is sometimes considered as an alternative consideration to that of justice. However, it is nonetheless rooted in ideas of justice. For one thing it rests on the assumption that everyone's well-being is equally important, and when we make our calculations about the maximizing of that well-being we must allocate equal importance to everyone. And by virtue of that it could be argued that it rests also on an idea of equality of importance between the providers of care resources and its recipients. In a public system of health and social care the resources for that care are provided ultimately by the taxpayer, locally and nationally. The justification for levying taxes for social and health care is that it is intended to improve the well-being of the population as a whole, and in particular of those in need. It is only in the interests of the taxpayer to pay taxes if those benefits are maximized. A commitment to utility is among other things a commitment to those taxpayers to ensure that the money they provide is used to achieve the maximum good possible. Any falling short of that goal is arguably a wasting of some part of those taxes and involves treating taxpayers as of secondary importance. So a commitment to utility implies equality between the givers and the receivers.

To some degree the component principles of distributive justice can be pursued in tandem, and to some degree choices have to be made between them. They can to varying degrees represent policy goals in their own right. I therefore propose to consider two of these principles further, in terms of their significance as policy goals in the context of prioritizing and rationing. The principles I have selected are utility and equality, as these seem to be most immediately relevant to the prevailing political and policy agenda. However the exclusions, need, rights and desert, require a word of explanation. Meeting needs presents some difficulties as a policy or political goal. This is because the definition of need is deeply problematic, both in terms of social and health care. The concept of need can be stretched or narrowed in accordance with resources, and this flexibility, as commented on by Blackman (1998), makes it less useful as a political goal than as an element in political rhetoric. Respect for rights presents a comparable problem. Positive rights enjoyed by the population are the cumulative results of government policy and legislation, so adherence to these would represent little more than passive maintenance on the part of government. If on the other hand government or other bodies were to seek to base their goals on ideal rights, they would find worse problems than those presented by the concept of need. Definitions of ideal rights in relation to health and social care are so debatable that they are of little help, again, outside the realm of political rhetoric. I have already indicated that desert seems not to be a relevant aspect of distributive justice in this context, and will therefore not receive further discussion. Instead I propose to consider another policy goal which is of particular relevance to the prevailing social and political climate, that of inclusion.

Utility

The principle of utility can be seen operating clearly as a policy and practice goal in health care. Medical practice is increasingly focused on selecting the best combination of treatment and patient in terms of success of outcome, and the development of evidence-based medicine has underpinned this commitment in recent years. Managers and planners are also explicitly committed to maximizing health gain per pound spent. And this influences priorities. One of the arguments against spending NHS money on in vitro fertilization is that its success rate as a treatment (or rather family of treatments) is relatively uneven compared with most established treatments used in the NHS. Likewise the choice of areas selected for priority under the Health of the Nation initiative was partly influenced by the likelihood of money being spent to good effect in those areas (DoH 1992). However, it shows much more starkly in rationing, where the degree of health gain predicted is the dominant guide for clinicians in deciding to provide or withhold treatment. Because one individual can benefit from a given treatment, it does not mean that he or she can benefit as much as another individual. The smoker may well benefit from the heart bypass operation, but on average will not benefit as much as the non-smoker, other things being equal. If there is only enough for one of those two individuals, the pressure must be on the first to lose out, as Underwood and Bailey (1993) point out, because a greater health gain can be achieved with the second.

The main problem with this principle is agreeing the most appropriate good to be pursued, and establishing definitions and indices of that good. The early utilitarians such as Bentham took a simple view that pleasure is the fundamental yardstick of utility (Bentham 1962), but the accretions of thinking since then have complicated this principle a good deal. In prioritizing by health care agencies, health gain is a term that is often used to define the main goal. Traditionally the indices of this have been life expectancy, infant mortality and general morbidity. However, it is clear that the 'good' that health care should be maximizing is not necessarily so simple, as Bowling's discussion makes clear (Bowling 1997). Quality of life as a 'good' has currency in contemporary culture and it is expressed in this context in the QALYs principle, which measures the improvement in quality of life achieved by a particular treatment for a particular person. However, quality of life does not necessarily coincide with health as it is normally understood. Increased car ownership undoubtedly contributes to individual quality of life in terms of opportunities and autonomy, despite its negative impact on both individual and community health. Frith (1999) argues that prioritizing cannot be based on scientific evidence of success because the nature of success is problematic, and is ultimately a question of value rather than of fact.

If we try to define the kind of utility gain appropriate for social care, the issues become even more difficult. At the basic level, health care can aim for reduction in mortality and morbidity. But social care has no equivalent even of that basic fall-back position. Social well-being is as nebulous a concept as one may wish to find. In essence, the function of moral values in defining what kind of social relationships are regarded as desirable is fully exposed in this context. The problem is further complicated by the fact that a full calculation of utility gained must be made on the basis of opportunity cost – that is, taking account of the utility lost by the fact that a given resource, by being devoted to the prioritized service, cannot be made available to the non-prioritized alternatives.

As far as rationing decisions are concerned the problem of definition of well-being also exists at the individual level where, at least in the case of people with serious or chronic illness, health status or prognosis may not always coincide with quality of life, and treatments which maintain life may reduce quality of life. To some degree QALYs addresses this problem, but even this does not resolve the difficulties of maximizing utility on the individual level. Dickenson (1999) argues that the medical approach to individual rationing decisions in health care, concerned with health gains for the individual patient, fails to take account of all the relevant utility considerations. For instance, the illness of one person has considerable impact on the well-being of others, and his or her prognosis and quality of life will in many cases be intertwined with the quality of other lives. So rationing guided by the utility of an individual patient may only take account of a portion of the total utility at stake. There is evidence that some GPs take some cognizance of the impact of a patient's illness on others (Crisp *et al.* 1997), but in public discussion of rationing procedures this element tends not to be seen as legitimate, and in any case it conflicts with the tradition in medical ethics that the doctor's responsibility to the individual patient has special status and ought not to be open to compromise with other relationships.

Equality

The unequal distribution of health and welfare – partly correlated with the unequal distribution of wealth – has been the target of prioritizing in a number of contexts. For instance, the government policy set out in the White Paper *Saving Lives: Our Healthier Nation* (DoH 1999) expresses a particular concern with inequality. The pre-1997 Conservative government was less concerned with this issue, but even in that era policies at a local level were pursing this goal. Because of its individualized nature, the making of individual rationing decisions does not lend itself to an egalitarian agenda. Equality in the *process* of deciding individual cases may be achievable, and this will be discussed below. But individual professionals can only achieve an equal distribution of resources within their own caseloads, which contributes little to general equality. Given the nature of medicine, the logic of which requires doctors to do their best for individual patients as they present themselves, the notion of aiming for equality of outcomes makes little sense. Where rationing decisions are made at team or patch level in social care, some equality can be aimed for within that compass, as described by Leat and Perkins (1998). But given the nature of social care needs, the kind of consistency of outcome that we might see as achieving equality would be both difficult and at odds with other goals. Interestingly the only method of rationing that genuinely works to maximize equality is the much-maligned waiting list. In its purest form it distributes the desired good equally between those seeking it by making everyone wait as nearly as possible the same length of time for it.

In terms of priorities, the equalizing of the distribution of health and social care would seem to be a realistic target to achieve, and the history of the past thirty years since the creation of RAWP in the 1970s has indicated the pursuit of this in relation to health care. History has also shown that progress can be reversed, as Whitehead (1994) suggests probably happened in the early 1990s with health care. But what was lost can presumably be retrieved. In the case of social care central government sought to create a framework for geographical equity of provision around the 1990 NHS and Community Care Act, but Blackman (1998) argues that there is still a good deal of inconsistency at the local authority level. There are good reasons in relation to distributive justice why access to health and social care should be as equal as possible. When people are suffering the effects of inequality, it could be argued that health and social care can offer a countervailing benefit, in several ways. First, the business of financing a public health and social care system out of progressive taxation involves the better-off paying more than the worse-off, without correspondingly greater access. This constitutes a movement of resources from the better-off to the worse-off. This might be seen in terms of a counterbalancing of inequality in the sense also that the worse-off tend to have worse health and greater need of health care and therefore benefit disproportionately in that sense also. A rather different perspective has been offered by Daniels (1985), who argues that if we are to ensure that people get a fair chance to compete in an unequal, competitive society, then certain of the goods that equip people to compete ought to be equally available. Education is one of these, and health and social care could be argued to be another.

A bigger problem arises if the target shifts from equality of health and social care to equality of health and social well-being. The goods which we seek to redistribute to achieve this equalization may not be the most effective in achieving that outcome. The issue of socioeconomic inequality of health which emerged in the early 1980s has been identified by government as a major focus of policy at the turn of the millennium (DoH 1999). It is still the case that people on lower incomes have more illness and shorter lives, but it is not clearly the case that changes in the delivery of health care are the most effective way of remedying this. Evidence is accumulating that other factors are at least as important in perpetuating these inequalities, and probably more so. As Wilkinson (1996) points out, unequal societies are also characterized by communities lacking in cohesion and solidarity, and social relationships characterized by mistrust and hostility. Those features bear most heavily on the worst-off in those societies, and there are strong correlations between that feature and the worse health of the worse-off. So this seems to be a societal problem. In the light of Arblaster *et al.*'s discussion (1996) it is open to doubt whether health care as it is at present understood is the best instrument for modifying this situation. Also it is hard to see how social care can make much of a difference if this is the real problem. There are possible exceptions to both these statements, in that health promotion in its more socially oriented form is at least aimed at some modification of social attitudes and relationships, and the same could be said for community and youth work. However, these activities are somewhat marginal still in terms of the total stock of resources of health and social care. In the case of health promotion Foster (1996) argues that it has no proven effectiveness in reducing health inequalities.

Inclusion

This is an additional policy goal which, though not generally regarded as part of the concept of distributive justice, represents a major concern in contemporary western societies, and has clear relevance for prioritizing and rationing issues. In health care the inclusion agenda is less developed than those of utility and equality. By contrast, there are clearly sectors of social care where it is a major goal.

By inclusion I mean the process whereby all members of a society feel a sense of full membership, in terms of opportunities to participate in socially and politically important activities, and the relevance of political and cultural processes to all members of the community. Social marginalization may be accompanied in many cases by social inequality, and often the losers in the socioeconomic pecking order are also the marginalized. But this does not mean that the two phenomena are the same. It is clear that many members of ethnic minorities feel marginalized, even when they have average or above-average incomes. It is possible for individuals to prosper materially and still feel that the institutions and activities central to their society are not relevant to them. The parts of the community whose situation is most relevant to this issue are those whose health and social care needs are in some way distinctive. Ethnic minorities are one example. The largest ethnic minorities have distinctive profiles in terms of morbidity and mortality (Ahmad 1993). Other minorities such as the gay community also have some relatively distinctive health needs. People with disabilities often have health needs of a particular sort. All these are minority groups who have some reasons to feel that their needs are not given sufficient priority because they are minorities. Inclusion interacts with the issue of equality. By virtue of their poverty and the disadvantages that accompany it, the poorest are also marginalized, and experience a real sense of social exclusion. The poor health of this group is simply the worst manifestation of the health inequality discussed earlier (Wilkinson 1996).

Prioritizing can work to an agenda of inclusion, and there are examples of the needs of particular minorities being given priority in terms of resourcing (Kenny *et al.* 1994). In terms of rationing, however, minorities are on the whole more likely to lose than gain by the rationing processes that are used in the National Health Service. As Lowe *et al.* (1995) point out, where rationing of 'mainstream' treatments and facilities aims to maximize utility, minorities whose needs do not fit comfortably with what is available are likely to be seen as less likely to benefit and as (unintentionally) discriminated against.

Conflicting goals

It is clear that the goals of maximizing well-being, achieving equality and achieving inclusion conflict with one another, actually or potentially. The general level of prosperity that has been achieved in western post-war capitalist economies is unprecedented. But one of the costs of achieving this has been the creation and perpetuation of a consistent proportion of the population who are materially disadvantaged. The speed and unevenness of change leaves individuals and communities marooned with insufficient skills and resources to participate in the general prosperity. That is the fundamental conflict between the maximization of well-being on the one hand, and the maximization of equality and inclusion on the other. Clearly this definition of well-being is a narrow one, focusing entirely on material prosperity; but it is arguably the globally dominant definition. In the context of health and social care conflicts between these goals are not so stark, but are nonetheless real. The business of enhancing the health status of the marginalized and disadvantaged is fraught with difficulties and uncertainties, and it can be reasonably argued that the return on investment of resources devoted to this end has been very variable indeed, and that money spent on the very disadvantaged and marginalized has often not been spent effectively (Foster 1996). In a sense this is not surprising. The problems of the underclass seem relatively intractable, and imperfectly understood. The cost-effectiveness of interventions may well be less than that of money spent on mainstream services where impacts and outcomes are more predictable. So we have an apparent conflict between the principle of maximizing well-being with every unit of resource used, on the one hand, and the principles of reducing inequality and marginalization on the other. It is uneconomical to help those who are hard to help.

However, this conflict is not a simple one. The goal of maximizing well-being of a population can be pursued independently of the level of well-being which that population experiences at the outset. It is possible to enhance the quality of any life, however rich and rewarding it may already be or however miserable it may be. The traditional utilitarian view would be that there is no moral difference between increasing the well-being of someone who is already well and happy, and increasing the well-being of someone who is unwell and unhappy. If the increases are equal in magnitude, then they are equal in moral worth and desirability. Clearly this offends against the egalitarian view. However, it can be argued, and has been argued by writers such as Rawls (1971), that this equation is a false one, and that in terms of the real resources required to make people's lives better, the demands of utility and equality flow together. This can be illustrated in money terms with an example from earlier in the chapter. For someone who is too poor to buy shoes and is faced with the prospect of physical privation and discomfort at that basic level, £40 offers the prospect of a good pair of shoes and solves a major practical problem, possibly for several years. For someone at the opposite end of the income hierarchy the impact of £40 will be largely lost. An extra bottle of good quality wine in a well-stocked cellar will barely be noticed. That individual's well-being is barely touched. So the same resources achieve widely differing accretions of well-being, depending on the starting level.

This principle seems to work well for income and material resources generally. It is less clear in other contexts, and in the health context there are situations where it does not seem to work so well. It may be less productive to spend resources on a very sick patient than on a less sick one. As Neuberger et al. (1998) point out, patients with serious diseases requiring major surgery (e.g. liver transplant, heart bypass) will tend to become less likely to benefit from that surgery, the more ill they are (which often means the longer they have been ill). They are more likely to die sooner than patients whose illness is less advanced. So here utility works against equality, in that it is more advantageous to help the better-off (i.e. less ill) rather than the worse-off patient.

Perhaps the same considerations can be applied to material deprivation. The kind of disadvantages that lead individuals to be so poor that
they cannot afford shoes may be in their own way as intractable as
chronic liver failure, just as resource-expensive to cure, and just as prone
to the kind of deterioration that I mentioned above in relation to chronic
illness, so that the long-term poor become more difficult to help
than the newly poor. It seems, then, that maximization of well-being
in a population – whether that well-being is physical or economic –
does not necessarily accord with the egalitarian goal of helping the
worst-off.

The conflict between the principles of equality and inclusion on the
one hand, and the maximizing of well-being on the other, is at one
level an obvious feature of contemporary politics, and one that western
societies have lived with for some time. However, it is useful to consider
the problems of prioritizing and rationing also in the context of the
more inclusive principle of distributive justice. The notion that it is
possible to distribute scarce resources in a just way, and that those in
control of the process should seek to be fair, provides a baseline for
evaluating both the process and the outcomes of prioritizing and rationing and also provides a wider context for the political goals I have
already discussed.

Justice in the mode of decision making

So far, the discussion has been primarily around the question of who
gets what, on the basis that a decision is just if it leads to a just allocation of resources. However, a second issue arises here, and that concerns
the *way* decisions are made – who makes them and how are they made.
Justice in the mode of decision making is in many respects as relevant as
justice in the outcome of the decision. A number of the established
principles of justice can be applied to the processes of rationing and
prioritizing. For instance, the Aristotelian principle of equal treatment of
those equal in relevant respects seems useful here. In rationing situations
patients should not be disadvantaged through characteristics that are
not directly relevant to the decision. For example, ethnicity would not
be relevant to most questions of health care prioritizing or rationing,
and it would be unjust to treat people of different ethnicities differently
in terms of decision-making process. An extension of this principle would
be a requirement for consistency – that different cases that are the same
in relevant respects should be dealt with in the same manner. In the
rationing context this would argue for the same protocols being used in
relation to patients who are relevantly similar, or for relevantly similar
patients to go onto the same waiting list. In the case of prioritizing the

principle of equality would apply to the treatment of different groups affected by prioritizing decisions. One requirement might be that particular groups should not exercise unequal influence over the process. The well-educated inhabitants of affluent rural areas ought not to be able to exercise unequal influence to prevent prioritizing of services to deprived and underserved mining villages. In terms of consistency of method we could take it that, for instance, a primary care trust should use the same process of consultation and decision making in relation to all its priorities, and in relation to all groups affected by its prioritizing. In rationing there is a particular risk of injustice arising where one criterion is used to stand in for another criterion. Age is sometimes used as a criterion for likelihood to benefit. Even race has, at least in isolated cases, been used to stand in for likelihood to benefit (Lowe *et al.* 1995). This is clearly unjust if race and age are not legitimate criteria, and people who are different in these respects are not *relevantly* different.

The second possible requirement is closely related to the first. It is that the decision makers should take account of all the relevant information in their decision. This requires that they have access to all the relevant information, and it also requires at a more fundamental level that there is agreement as to what information is relevant. Agreement is also required as to what the criteria of distributive justice are, and what their relative importance is. The importance of information about a patient's life expectancy will depend on the importance we give to the principle of utility as a criterion of distributive justice. This must mean that we cannot realistically hope for a complete consensus on what information is relevant in any given case, because we are unlikely to achieve agreement as to the relative weight of utility, need and rights.

The third arguable requirement for processual justice is one of transparency. Decisions should be open to scrutiny by those affected, or by their representatives. Here the situations with regard to rationing and prioritizing are very different. Rationing, as an activity that is generally individual in its focus, and implemented by clinicians and administrators, cannot reasonably be expected to be open to unrestricted public scrutiny in every case because the privacy of individual patients would thereby be breached. A system of confidential audit of rationing decisions by a public body would overcome this problem, but at present professional boundaries, primarily those of the medical profession, prevent this. However, the development of clinical governance in the health service may provide an element of consistent scrutiny of such decisions. For prioritizing decisions there is no real excuse for invisible decision making in bodies which are accountable to government or the electorate, and again the Oregon experiment provides a good example both of the possibilities of open decision making and its difficulties. Also, Hutton's recommendations (2000) may provide a model for this.

Conclusion

Rationing and prioritizing in health and social care provide a useful reference point for a democratic society in exposing the nature of resourcing dilemmas in a particularly clear and accessible way. The conflicting principles that feature in this area are not greatly different from the principles that relate to other areas in which goods must be distributed, and the open discussion of cases and issues in health and social care has great potential in terms of the education of the public, as well as of planners, politicians and professionals. So we might hope that as these issues are discussed, public debate will become better informed and more balanced. As deference disappears from our culture and the public become less willing to accept decisions by doctors or managers on the basis of status alone, that process of education becomes vitally necessary if our public health care system is to retain its legitimacy. This is not to say that the public will necessarily wish to be directly involved in prioritizing decisions or to influence rationing decisions. The emotive nature of such decisions and the weight of responsibility involved may well continue to act as a repellent in that respect. But greater assertiveness and greater confidence on the part of the public is likely to express itself in a demand for methods of decision making that are transparently fair in their methods, even if outcomes will always remain problematic.

References

Ahmad, W. (1993) *'Race' and Health in Contemporary Britain*. Buckingham: Open University Press.

Arblaster, L., Lambert, M., Entwhistle, V. *et al.* (1996) A systematic review of the effectiveness of health service interventions aimed at reducing inequalities in health, *Journal of Health Service Research and Policy*, 1: 93–103.

Baker, R. (1993) Visibility and the just allocation of health care: a study of age rationing in the British National Health Service. *Health Care Analysis*, 1: 139–50.

Bentham, J. (1962) Introduction to the principles of morals and legislation, in M. Warnock (ed.) *Utilitarianism*. London: Collins.

Blackman, T. (1998) Facing up to underfunding: equity and retrenchment in community care, *Social Policy and Administration*, 32: 182–95.

Bowling, A. (1997) *Measuring Health: A Review of Quality of Life Measurement Scales*, 2nd edn. Buckingham: Open University Press.

Court, C. (1995) Survey shows widespread rationing in NHS, *British Medical Journal*, 311: 1453–4.

Crisp, R., Hope, T. and Ebbs, D. (1997) The Asbury Draft Policy on Ethical Use of Resources, in B. New (ed.) *Rationing Talk and Action*. London: Kings Fund.

Daniels, N. (1985) *Just Health Care*. New York, NY: Cambridge University Press.

Dickenson, D. (1999) Can medical criteria settle priority-setting debates? *Health Care Analysis*, 7: 131–7.

DoH (Department of Health) (1992) *The Health of the Nation: A Strategy for Health in England*. London: HMSO.

DoH (Department of Health) (1999) *Saving Lives: Our Healthier Nation*. London: HMSO.

Doyal, L. and Gough, I. (1991) *A Theory of Human Need*. London: Macmillan.

Ellis, K., Davis, A. and Rummary, K. (1999) Needs assessment, street-level bureaucracy and the new community care, *Social Policy and Administration*. 33: 262–80.

Ferriman, A. (1999) UK government finalises restrictions on Viagra prescribing, *British Medical Journal*, 318: 1305.

Foster, P. (1996) Inequalities and health: what health systems can and cannot do, *Journal of Health Service Research and Policy*, 1: 179–82.

Frith, L. (1999) Priority-setting and evidence-based purchasing, *Health Care Analysis*, 7: 139–51.

Government Committee on Choices in Health Care (1992) *Choices in Health Care*. Rijswijk: Minstry of Welfare, Health and Cultural Affairs.

Gray, A. and Jenkins, B. (1995) Public management and the National Health Service, in J. Glynn and D. Perkins (eds) *Managing Health Care: Challenges for the 90s*. London: Saunders.

Ham, C. (1999) *Health Policy in Britain: The Politics and Organisation of the National Health Service*, 4th edn. Basingstoke: Macmillan.

Harris, J. (1991) Unprincipled QALYs: a response to Gibbon, *Journal of Medical Ethics*, 17: 185–8.

Hope, T., Sprigings, D. and Crisp, R. (1993) 'Not clinically indicated': patients' interests or resource allocation? *British Medical Journal*, 306: 379–81.

Hope T., Hicks, N., Reynolds, D., Crisp, R. and Griffiths, S. (1998) Rationing and the health authority, *British Medical Journal*, 317: 1067–9.

Hunter, D. (1997) *Desperately Seeking Solutions*. London: Addison-Wesley-Longman.

Hurley, J., Birch, S., Stoddart, G. and Torrance, G. (1997) Medical necessity, benefit and resource allocation in health care, *Journal of Health Service Research and Policy*, 2: 223–8.

Hutton, W. (2000) *New Life for Health: The Commission on the NHS*. London: Vintage.

Judge, K. (1978) *Rationing Social Services: A Study of Resource Allocation in the Personal Social Services*. London: Heinemann.

Kenny, C., Qurban, A. and Cassidy, D. (1994) *A Review of the Needs of People from Black and Minority Ethnic Groups in Southern Derbyshire*. Derby: Southern Derbyshire Health Authority and Derbyshire Family Health Services Authority.

Kitzhaber, J. (1993) Prioritising health services in an era of limits: the Oregon experience, *British Medical Journal*, 307: 373–7.

Klein, R., Day, P. and Redmayne, S. (1996) *Managing Scarcity*. Buckingham: Open University Press.

Leat, D. and Perkins, E. (1998) Juggling and dealing: the creative work of care package purchasing, *Social Policy and Administration*, 32: 166–81.

Lightfoot, J. (1995) Identifying needs and setting priorities: issues of theory, policy and practice, *Health and Social Care in the Community*, 3: 105–14.

Lowe, M., Kerridge, I. and Mitchell, K. (1995) 'These sorts of people don't do very well': race and allocation of health care resources, *Journal of Medical Ethics*, 21: 356–60.

Mill, J. S. (1962) Utilitarianism, in M. Warnock (ed.) *Utilitarianism*. London: Collins.

Miller, D. (1976) *Social Justice*. Oxford: Clarendon.

Neuberger, J., Adams, D., McMaster, P., Maidment, A. and Speed, M. (1998) Assessing priorities for allocation of donor liver grafts: survey of public and clinicians, *British Medical Journal*, 317: 172–5.

New, B. (1997) *Rationing Talk and Action*. London: Kings Fund.

Paton, H. J. (1978) *The Moral Law: Kant's 'Groundwork of the Metaphysic of Morals'*. London: Hutchinson.

Pickard, S. and Sheaff, R. (1999) Primary care groups and NHS rationing, *Health Care Analysis*, 7: 37–56.

Rawls, J. (1971) *A Theory of Justice*. Cambridge, MA: Harvard University Press.

Redmayne, S. and Klein, R. (1993) Rationing in practice: the case of in vitro fertilisation, *British Medical Journal*, 306: 1521–4.

Richardson, R. and Waddington, C. (1996) Allocating resources: community involvement is not easy, *International Journal of Health Planning and Management*, 11: 307–15.

Small, N. (1990) *Politics and Planning in the National Health Service*. Buckingham: Open University Press.

Smith, L. and Morrissey, J. (1994) Ethical dilemmas for general practitioners under the UK new contract, *Journal of Medical Ethics*, 20: 175–80.

Smith, R. (1993) Conference agrees on need to ration but not on how, *British Medical Journal*, 306: 737.

Toon, P. (1994) Justice for gatekeepers, *Lancet*, 343: 585–7.

Underwood, M. and Bailey, J. (1993) Coronary bypass surgery should not be offered to smokers, *British Medical Journal*, 306: 1047–50.

Whitehead, M. (1994) Who cares about equity in the NHS? *British Medical Journal*, 308: 1284–7.

Wilkinson, R. (1996) *Unhealthy Societies*. London: Routledge.

Williams, A. (1985) Economics of coronary artery bypass grafting, *British Medical Journal*, 291: 326–9.

chapter **ten**

CONCLUSION

Since Labour's winning of a second term in the UK general election of 2001 the main health and social policy debate has been over the future role and funding of public services. Whereas the 'third way' put stress on enlarging the function of local communities and on re-establishing links between rights and responsibilities, Labour's modernization project for the NHS, education and local government appears only achievable by strengthening the power of the centre. Modernizing tendencies which weaken the basis of old-style municipal socialism encourage public–private partnerships, contracting out of public services by local government and the transfer of council houses to social landlords. The argument follows that if national standards are to be achieved across the country; and if 'postcode rationing' is to cease, new instruments have to be devised for controlling the activities of local public services such as health trusts, schools, police and transport. Following the introduction of performance indicators in the 1980s and the creation of a more hierarchical management system in the 1990s, all public services are to be subjected to even more powerful instruments of central control.

Public Private Partnerships (PPP) involve government plans to bring private companies into the heart of health, education and other areas. They have been somewhat precariously defended by ministers as the debate continues within political and other quarters over what exact role the private sector will eventually play. PPP is an arrangement, mostly long-term, under which the public and private sector work closely together to achieve a clearly defined common purpose (PPPs take many forms, including concessions, franchises and joint ventures). It derives from the privatization process when the Conservative government in the early 1990s began to force local town hall public services to be subject to compulsory competitive tendering. Then chancellor Norman Lamont created the Public Finance Initiative to offer a design, build, finance and operate a particular model, which is now but one of a variety of PPPs. These ideas came to fruition in the mid-1990s with a number of road and prison schemes. New Labour wishes to increase spending on public infrastructure without resorting too heavily towards public funding for overall costs. A special taskforce established by the Treasury has helped to drive the concept forward.

Tony Blair, speaking at the public services union Unison's annual conference, asserted that 'he was not talking about privatizing the public services but rather their better delivery' (*Guardian*, 12 July 2001). This has always been the message from the Prime Minister. However, recurring figures demonstrating poor achievements of targets will likely justify further assignations with the private sector. Figures between April and September 2001, for example, disclosed that despite extra billions being poured into the health service this has failed to produce any significant increase in the number of hospital patients being treated. NHS spending increased from £44.2 billion in 2000/01 to £48 billion for the following year. Although much of this increase will have gone into higher pay, costlier drugs and better facilities, the government's objective was to reduce average waiting times.

The concept of partnership has been dealt with in detail in Chapter 6. Among statutory organizations (and, indeed, among voluntary and private organizations as well) this is a key theme of current UK government policy (Glendinning *et al.* 2001). Health and social policies are delivered through means of programmes and plans built around targets which require partnerships as the instrument for meeting such targets. It is within the provision of health and social services that principal opportunities for partnership working are expected to emerge. The NHS White Paper *The New NHS: Modern, Dependable* (DoH 1997) repeatedly urged NHS and local authority organizations to work more closely together. This was formalized in the 'duty of partnership' imposed by the 1999 Health Act on all NHS organizations and supported by a number of other policy and funding initiatives. Conversely, the Local Government Act 2000 empowers local authorities to work in partnership with other local agencies to improve economic, social and environmental well-being. At a strategic level, partnerships between health and local authorities are underpinned by the latter's contribution to the development and implementation of local Health Improvement Plans (HImPs) (DoH 1997); by the requirement to cooperate in local leadership of national service priorities (DoH 1998); and in the preparation of Joint Investment Plans for older people and other user groups (DoH 2000). Grants from the Social Services Modernization Fund have been 'ring-fenced' for partnership development between health and social services organizations (DoH 1999); and flexibilities introduced by the 1999 Health Act allow health and local authority organizations to pool budgets, delegate commissioning responsibilties to a single 'lead' organization and integrate front-line health and social service professionals in a single organization (Hudson *et al.* 2001). *The NHS Plan* (DoH 2000b) proposed closer operational links between health and social services staff; a range of financial incentives and rewards for joint working; and new partnership bodies, 'care trusts', whose governance arrangements will reflect equal health and social services involvement, which can commission and provide integrated health and social services (DoH 2001). Where collaboration is judged inadequate or ineffective, powers in the Health and Social Care Act 2001 will give the Secretary of State powers to impose partnerships on reluctant local partners.

The health policies of the Labour government 1997–2001 included an increased emphasis on the contribution of social services departments (SSDs) to promoting health involving the drive towards organizational fusion between elements of the NHS and SSDs; new mechanisms for conjoint funding of health and social services; and a policy focus on tackling health inequalities by combating social inequalities on a national and locality basis (Bywaters and McLeod 2001). At the front line, the development of practice strategies and frameworks are increasingly removing or overriding the separate identities and approaches of health and local authorities. The NHS Plan stated that a single health and social care assessment and care planning process will be introduced by April 2002, initially for older people who are most vulnerable (para. 15.9). Locally based projects, such as Sure Start, require both the development of new joint services and the coordination and streamlining of existing local authority and community and primary health care services. Recent policy announcements also imply that social services staff will increasingly be located in multidisciplinary teams outside their departments. Partnership that involves effective community participation is likely to produce better results. The impact to date of community involvement on regeneration has generally been modest and commitment to community involvement has often been tokenistic. Good practice in this field of work shows that communities have a fresh perspective and can often see the problem in new ways; community involvement helps to deliver programmes which more accurately target local needs; the resulting projects are more acceptable to the local community; programme outputs which have been designed with input from local residents are likely to last longer (JRF 1999).

The definition of partnership is problematic, for example if it is to be measured (the OED defines partnership as an association/undertaking among two or more people with shared risks and profits). It is when agencies (statutory, voluntary, private) through their representatives work on 'cross-cutting issues'; where such agencies involve 'communities' and there is working together to produce 'joined-up' solutions addressing local problems relating to health, education, employment, crime and disorder and social inclusion (Home Office 1991; DoH 1998; Social Exclusion Unit 1998; Cabinet Office 1999). It infers integration, in preference to collaboration, through means such as pooled agency budgets, identifying lead commissioning and joint mission statements; and also a substantial degree of commitment and trust on the part of participating agencies. Finally, partnership infers involving communities through creating structures that work for local communities, making resources available for community groups, arranging training for both community activists and professionals and helping community groups with administrative and financial procedures.

This book has attempted to articulate some of the tensions and background debate to framing health and social policies. As for the future, user involvement and service user movements are likely to persist as the main source of challenge, as are policies for tackling poverty and social exclusion. The approach will be on identifying best practice, applying findings from research more widely and discovering effective means for rebuilding a depleted workforce within, in particular, health, social care and educational provision. Robust, long-term strategies are required in this regard in order to combat under-recruitment, skill shortage and low pay combined with a broader commitment to maintaining public services. Such services should have a civilizing function and endeavour to promote tolerance and understanding among different social groupings.

References

Bywaters, P. and McLeod, E. (2001) The impact of New Labour health policy on social services: a new deal for service users' health? *British Journal of Social Work*, 31: 579–94.

Cabinet Office (1999) *Modernising Government*, Cm 4310. London: The Stationery Office.

DoH (Department of Health) (1997) *The New NHS: Modern, Dependable*. London: The Stationery Office.

DoH (Department of Health) (1998) *Modernising Health and Social Services: National Priorities Guidance 1999/00–2001/02*. London: Department of Health.

DoH (Department of Health) (1999) *Promoting Independence: Partnership, Prevention and Carers Grants – Conditions and Allocations 1999/2000*, LAC (99) 13. London: Department of Health.

DoH (Department of Health) (2000a) Joint Investment Plans, Health and Social Care Joint Unit, Department of Health, www.doh.gov, UK/joint, updated 12 January 2000.

DoH (Department of Health) (2000b) *The NHS Plan. A Plan for Investment, a Plan for Reform*. Cm 4818–1. London: HMSO.

DoH (Department of Health) (2001) Care Trusts: Emerging Framework, http://www.doh.gov.uk/caretrusts/index.htm, updated 14 March 2001.

Glendinning, C., Abbott, S. and Coleman, A. (2001) 'Bridging the gap': new relationships between primary care groups and local authorities, *Social Policy and Administration*, 35 (4): 411–25.

Home Office (1991) *Safer Communities: The Local Delivery of Crime Prevention Through the Partnership Approach*. London: The Stationery Office.

Hudson, B., Young, R., Hardy, B. and Glendinning, C. (2001) *National Evaluation of Notifications for Use of the Section 31 Partnership Flexibilities of the Health Act 1999: Interim Report*. Leeds: Nuffield Institute for Health/Manchester: National Primary Care Research and Development Centre.

JRF (Joseph Rowntree Foundation) (1999) *Developing Effective Community Involvement Strategies (Guidance for Single Regeneration Budget Bids)*. York: Joseph Rowntree Foundation.

Social Exclusion Unit (1998) *Bringing Britain Together: A National Strategy for Neighbourhood Renewal*, Cm 4045. London: The Stationery Office.

INDEX

Abel-Smith, B., 68, 69
accidents, risk of, 29–30
accountability, 77, 95–6
Adams, R., 61, 62
agency, 36–7
  and consumerism, 36, 37, 41
  expressive, 36–7
  historical background, 34
  political, 8
agency theory, 89
Ahmad, W., 112–13, 153
Alaszewski, A., 20–1, 103
  and Manthorpe, J., 123, 131, 133
anti-discriminatory practice, 129
autonomy, 33, 34, 36, 37, 71
  professional, attacks on, 94–5

Barnes, M.
  and Bowl, R., 61
  and Prior, D., 115–16
  and Warren, L., 63
Beck, U., 7, 23
Bentham, J., 69, 149
Best Value, 56, 130
Beveridge, W., 112, 114–15, 116, 117
Black Report, 53
Blackman, T., 145, 148, 151
Blair, Tony, 6–7, 8, 10, 161
'bounded rationality', 79
Bowling, A., 128, 149
Bradshaw, P., 98
Bryson, J. M., 66, 67
Buckinghamshire County Council, 61
Bunton, R. and Burrows, R., 40, 128

capitalism, 36, 41, 70–1
  Marxist analysis, 34–5
care management and assessment, DoH
  guidance, 58, 60
Care Standards Act (2000), 58
carers, informal, 117–20
Carer's National Strategy, 119
Caring for People (Secretaries of State), 57,
  103
Central Office of Information, 52
Chadwick, R., 28
Challis, L. et al., 100
'change agents', 91
child care role, women, 114–16, 117–18
child protection, 24–5, 101, 129
Child Support Acts (1991/5), 115, 116
Child Support Agency, 46
Childcare Tax Credit, 9
childhood accident rate, 29–30
CHImp, see Commission for Health
  Improvement
choice, 59–61, 119
citizen participation, 45
Citizen's Charters, 55–6
citizens' panels, 14
citizenship, and consumerism, 56
civil society, 47, 48
Clarke, J., 110, 125
  and Newman, J., 84, 88, 89, 91, 92
clinical governance, 80, 134, 156
collaboration, 102
collectivism
  vs individualism, 33–4
  see also solidarity

Commission for Health Improvement
(CHImp), 11, 14
communitarianism, 6, 13, 44–5
community, 12–13, 46–8
community care, *see* NHS and Community
Care Act (1990); social care
Community Care (Direct Payments) Act
(1996), 62
complaints system, 57–8
conflicting goals, 153–5
conflicting principles, 1–4
Conservative government, *see* Thatcherism
consumerism/consumers, 54–7
  and agency, 36, 37, 41
  and capitalism, 36, 41
  and citizenship, 56
  and empowerment, 2, 61–3
  health care, 39–40, 55, 95
  historical background, 51–4
  social care, 40, 41, 57–61
continuous quality improvement (CQI),
  133, 134
cooperative relationships, 78, 80, 135
cost-effectiveness
  and equity, 69
  of health care, 127, 128
  health promotion, 145–6
  of social care, 129–30
costs of caring, 120
Cronin, J. E., 44, 70
*Cross-Departmental Review of Provision for
  Young Children* (DfEE), 13
'culture management', 91
culture of quality assurance, 133–4

Daniels, N., 72, 144, 151
David, M., 56
decision making
  rationing, 155–6
  risk, 24–30
Dennis, N., 38, 46, 47
Department of Education (DfEE), 13
Department of the Environment (DoE), 26,
  27
Department of Health (DoH), 10, 21, 161–2
  inter-agency working, 101, 102
  practitioners' guidance on care
    management and assessment, 58, 60
  see also specific publications
Department of Health and Social Security
  (DHSS), 119
Department of Social Security (DSS), 9
dependence of women, 114
deserving/undeserving poor, 52–3
  see also entitlement
dialectic materialism, 1
direct payments, 62–3, 119
disabled people, 62–3, 113, 117–18, 153

distributive justice, 144–8
Douglas, M., 18
Driver, S. and Martell, L., 6, 12, 45

ecological issues, *see* environmental issues
education, multidisciplinary, 102–3
education policy, 13, 56
Ellis, K., 59
  et al., 144, 147
Ellis, R. and Whittington, D., 125, 127
empowerment, 2, 58, 61–3
English National Board (ENB), 103
Enthoven, A., 75, 94
entitlement, 146–7
  see also deserving/undeserving poor
environmental issues, 8
environmental policy, 26
equality
  conflicting goals, 153–5
  and cost-effectiveness, 69
  and decision making, 155–6
  gender, 116–17
  and inclusion, 43, 153–5
  of outcome, 42
  and prioritizing/rationing, 144–6, 150–2,
    155–6
ethnic minorities, 112–13, 153, 155
Etzioni, A., 6
expressive agency, 36–7

family
  forms, 110–16
  parental responsibility, 56
  policy, 116–17
  responsibility for, 37–8
  roles, 13, 40–1, 45–6
  values, 13
  see also women
Family and Disabled Children Act (2000),
  119
fertility, 111, 112, 149
Field, Frank, 9–10
Fish, D. and Coles, C., 87–8
Foster, P., 145–6, 152, 153–4
  and Wilding, P., 92, 94, 95
'fright factors', 22
funding issues, 161–2

gender
  equity, 116–17
  see also women
general practitioners (GPs), 94–5, 150
  fundholders, 55, 77–8, 131, 142–3
genetic screening, 27–8
genetics, decision making, 26–8
Giddens, A., 5–8, 23, 36–7, 40, 45
Gilligan, C., 117
Gladstone, D., 83

Glendenning, C., 95, 120
  et al., 62–3, 161
Glennerster, H., 55, 59, 75, 77–8, 115, 131
globalization, 7
Goldmann, D., 133, 134
Gray, A. and Jenkins, B., 77, 141–2
Gray, J., 33, 35, 71
Griffiths, R., 74, 85, 93–4
Growing Older (DHSS), 119

Habermas, J., 36, 80
Ham, C., 14, 68, 73, 79, 141
Harris, J., 112, 114, 116, 143
Harrison, S.
  et al., 68, 94
  and Pollitt, C., 94
Health (Service) Act (1999), 135, 161–2
health care
  influences, 125
  planning and competition, 72–4
  quality assurance in, 126–9
  rationing in, 142–3
  Thatcherism and, 38–40
health economics, 128, 143
Health Improvement Plans (HImPs), 161
Health of the Nation, The (DoH), 39, 41,
  128, 149
health promotion, 39–40, 42–3, 48, 128–9
  cost-effectiveness, 145–6
Health and Social Care Act (2001), 162
HImPs, see Health Improvement Plans
Hudson, B., 72, 100, 101
Hugman, R., 86, 102
Human Fertilisation and Embryology
  Authority, 28
Human Genetics Advisory Commission, 28
Human Rights Act (1998), 26, 147
Hunter, D., 79, 102, 134–5, 139, 141
Hutton, W., 6, 8, 35, 39, 156

ill health
  impact on well-being of others, 150
  and poverty, 53, 152, 153, 155
  utility vs equality principle, 154
inclusion, 152–3
  equality and, 43, 153–5
incremental planning, 68–9
individual responsibility, see responsibility
individual rights, see rights
individualism, 7–8
  vs collectivism, 33–4
  historical background, 34–5
  policy and politics, 37–8
  recent developments, 35–6
informal carers, 117–20
information, 68, 76–7, 156
inter-agency working, 101, 102
internal market, 39, 74–9

Johnson, N., 11, 13
'joined-up' approaches, 13, 100
joint consultative committees (JCC), 12
Joint Investment Plans, 161
'joint practitioner' service, 15
'juggling' work and care, 111
justice
  in decision making, 155–6
  distributive, 144–8

Kant, I., 32, 33, 34, 37, 144–5
King's Fund, 143
Klein, R., 66–7, 73, 79, 93, 94, 95, 128,
  133, 134
  et al., 139, 140–1
knowledge, professional, 85–7
Krieger, J., 44, 71

Labour, see New Labour; third way
Lamont, Norman, 161
lay membership of professional bodies, 14
Le Grand, J., 6, 9, 28
  and Bartlett, W., 55, 89
learning disabilities, 60, 61
  nursing, 103
Leat, D. and Perkins, E., 144, 151
left/right distinction, 8
legislation, 44
  see also specific Acts
Lewis, J., 114
liberal state, 43–4
  see also neo-liberalism
Light, D., 76, 78
Lippman, A., 28
Lister, R., 42, 55
Local Authority Social Services Act (1970),
  54
Local Government Act (2000), 161
Longcare Inquiry, 61
Lowe, M. et al., 153, 156

Macdonald, K., 85, 86
Malin, N. et al., 15, 101
managerialism, 88–92, 127
Manthorpe, J.
  Alaszewski, A. and, 123, 131, 133
  and Phillips, J., 111
  Stanley, N. and, 24, 119
market competition, 39, 74–8
  New Labour response, 78–9
  and quality assurance, 134–5
  quasi-market reforms, 55, 75, 89
  see also planning, and competition
Marxism, 1, 33, 34–5
maximizing equality, 153–4
maximizing inclusion, 153–4
maximizing well-being, 147–8, 155–6
Maxwell, R. J., 125, 133

medical audit, 127
medical profession
  attacks on autonomy, 93–5
  foreign trained doctors, 98
  influence of, 125
  rationing in health care, 142–3
  scrutiny of practice, 127–8, 133
medicine, 125, 128
mental health
  and family life, 113, 119
  models, 126
  risk assessment, 24
  teamwork, 103
  third way approach, 12–13
Mental Health Act (1983), 60
Mental Health Foundation, 60
Merkle, J., 89
Mill, J. S., 33, 70, 147–8
Millar, J., 46, 112
Miller, D., 144, 145, 146
Modernising Social Services (DoH), 11–12, 98, 100
modernization, 95–9, 160
  NHS Plan, 14–15, 96–8, 162
  third way, 11–13, 160
multidisciplinary education, 102–3
Munro, E., 24–5

National Commission for Care Standards, 58
National Health Service, *see* NHS
National Institute of Clinical Excellence (NICE), 11, 14, 95
National Service Frameworks (NSFs), 11, 13
National Training Organisation for Personal Social Services (TOPSS), 99
needs, 145, 148
  distinctive, 153
  layers and levels, 145–6
  social insurance, women, 114
neo-liberalism, 71, 72–3
  see also consumerism; liberal state; Thatcherism
Neuberger, J. *et al.*, 147, 154
New Contract for Welfare: New Ambitions for our Country, A (DSS), 9
New Labour, 3–4
  approach to community, 47–8
  approach to family, 46
  organizational fusion, 162
  response to internal market, 78–9
  responsibility *vs* solidarity, 41–3, 44–5
  see also modernization; third way
New National Health Service; Modern, Dependable, The (DoH), 10–11, 95, 100, 161
New Right, 37–8, 43, 45, 46, 92

NHS
  Conservative reforms, 35, 38–40, 55–6, 127, 132, 142–3
  creation of, 52, 73
  development of quality assurance, 126–7
  fertility treatment, 149
  Griffiths Report, 74, 85, 93–4
  internal market, 39, 74–9
  New Labour reforms, 10–11, 14–15, 42–3, 56–7
  planning, 73–4
  primary care-led, 102
  spending increases, 161
NHS and Community Care Act (1990), 21
  complaints system, 57–8
  inter-agency working, 103
  quality assurance agenda, 127
  quasi-market reforms, 55
  rationing, 143, 144, 146, 151
  social care agenda, 40, 57, 129–30, 151
NHS Plan, 14–15, 96–8, 162
NHS Primary Care Act (1997), 95
NICE, *see* National Institute of Clinical Excellence
No Secrets (DoH), 61
NSFs, *see* National Service Frameworks
nursing
  Griffiths recommendations, 93
  influence of profession, 125, 127
  learning disabilities, 103
  NHS Plan, 97, 98
  as semi-profession, 86–7

obligation, 146–7
older people, 63, 119–20, 146–7
organizations
  fusion of, 162
  impact of quality assurance, 132–5
  professional, lay/citizen membership of, 14
  voluntary, 41, 47

parental responsibility, 56
Parent's Charter, 56
partnership, 161–3
  joint consultative committees (JCC), 12
  and professionalism, 100–3
patient(s)
  -as-citizen, 39–40
  as consumers, 55, 95
  -professional power relations, 52
  role, 38–9
Patient's Charter (DoH), 95
Paton, H. J., 10–11, 37, 144–5
patriarchy, 86
PCGs, *see* primary care groups

planning
  and competition, 2, 67–8, 72–4
    historic and political background,
      69–72
  levels, 68–9
Pollitt, C., 91, 134
  Harrison, S. and, 94
Poor Law, 51, 54
post-Fordism, 123–4
poverty
  and childhood accident rate, 29–30
  and ill health, 53, 152, 153, 155
  Sure Start programme, 13
Powell, M., 8, 9, 116–17
  and Hewitt, M., 41
power relations, 52–3, 85, 131
PPP, see Public Private Partnerships
practitioners' guidance on care
      management and assessment (DoH),
      58, 60
primary care groups (PCGs), 10–11,
      143
primary care-led NHS, 102
Prior, L., 132–3
Prior, P. M., 113
prioritizing/rationing
  in context, 141–4
  definitions, 139–41
  equality, 144–6, 150–2, 155–6
  in health care, 142–3
  in social care, 144
  see also justice; utility principle
professionalism, 84–8
  and accountability, 95–6
  conflicting views of, 87–8
  and partnership, 100–3
professions
  political attacks on, 92–5
  views of carers, 118–19
Promoting Better Health (DoH), 39
Public Finance Initiative, 161
Public Private Partnerships (PPP), 160–1
purchaser/provider split, 55, 94
Putnam, R., 23

quality
  definitions/concepts, 131, 133
  measurement, 130–1
quality assurance
  approaches to, 131
  culture of, 133–4
  in health care, 126–9, 132
  impact of, 131–5
    between organizations, 134–5
    within organizations, 132–4
  and market competition, 134–5
  problems and issues, 130–1
  in social care, 129–30, 132–3

Quality Strategy for Social Care, A (DoH),
      98–9
quality-adjusted life years (QALYS), 94,
      143, 149, 150
quasi-consumers, 55, 58
quasi-market reforms, 55, 75, 89

rational planning, 68, 73–4
rationality, 33, 34
  'bounded', 79
  in decision making, 89, 90–1
  and irrationality, 35
rationing, see prioritizing/rationing
Rawls, J., 43–4, 144, 154
Resource Allocation Working Party
      (RAWP), 73, 141, 151
Resource allocation, see prioritizing/
      rationing
responsibility
  and agency, 37
  for health, 38–40
  parental, 56
  and rights, 6–7, 9
'responsible consumer', 57
rights
  Human Rights Act (1998), 26
  ideal/moral and positive, 146–7,
      148
  and responsibilities, 6–7, 9
  women's, 28, 116–17
risk, 7
  balance of, 23–4
  decision making, 24–30
  defining and redefining, 18–20
  external and manufactured, 23
  positive and negative outcomes,
      19–20
  and trust, 23–4
  as vulnerability, 20–2
'risky behaviour', 28
Roberts, H. *et al.*, 29–30

Samuelson, P., 67
Saving Lives: Our Healthier Nation (DoH), 43,
      45, 46, 150, 152
SCIE, see Social Care Institute for
      Excellence
scientific management, 89–90
Seebohm Committee, 54
Self, P., 90, 91
'semi-professions', 86
Sennett, R., 36, 102
service users (social care), 57–61
Simon, H., 90–1
single mothers, 114–16
Small, N., 73, 141
Smith, R., 66, 146, 143
social capital, 23

social care
  Conservative policies, 40–1, 46, 58
  influences, 111, 125–6
  New Labour policies, 11–13, 41–3
  planning and competition, 72–4
  quality assurance in, 129–30
  rationing in, 144
Social Care Institute for Excellence (SCIE),
  98–9
social changes, 34–5
  impact on family, 111–16
  impact on women, 110–12
social class, *see* poverty
social democracy, 71–2
'social exclusion', 8–9
Social Exclusion Unit, 9, 10, 19–20, 100,
  114–15
social insurance needs, women,
  114
social security claimants, 52–4
social services departments (SSDs),
  162
Social Services Modernization Fund,
  161–2
social workers, 86, 97–9
solidarity
  and agency, 37
  New Labour policies, 41–3, 44–5
  vs individualism, 33–4
staff issues, NHS Plan, 14–15
  recruitment, 97–8
state models, 43–5
'subsidiarity' principle, 77
Sure Start programme, 13, 162

Tawney, R. H., 34
teamwork, 102, 103
technical-rational view of professionalism,
  87
teenage pregnancy, 19–20, 114–15
Thatcherism, 2–3, 35, 38
  and health, 38–40
  and social care, 40–1, 46, 58

third way, 5–11
  dilemmas, 7–8
  modernization and social provision,
    11–13
  NHS Plan, 14
  women's rights, 116–17
TOPSS, *see* National Training Organisation
  for Personal Social Services
transparency, 156
trust, and risk, 23–4

United Nations Charter of Human Rights,
  146
users (social care), 57–61
utility principle, 69–70, 145, 147–8,
  149–50, 154

voluntary organizations, 41, 47
voucher systems, 54–5, 59, 119
vulnerable groups, 20–2, 54

waiting lists, 144
welfare state, 2–3, 8–10
welfare-to-work programme, 9–10, 11–12
Whitehead, M., 141, 151
Wilkinson, R., 152, 153
Williams, A., 41, 47, 143
women
  care roles, 40–1, 114–16, 117–20
  in caring professions, 86–7
  concept of dependence, 114
  costs of caring, 120
  family stresses, 113–14
  mental health problems, 113
  rights, 28, 116–17
  single mothers, 114–16
  social changes and, 110–12
  social insurance needs, 114
Working Families Tax Credit, 9
Working for Patients (DoH), 55, 94
Wright, Tony, 95–6

You and Your Child's Education, 56